Lifesav
For Your M

Practical Easy-To-Use Ideas To Strengthen Your Marriage

by

Mack and Brenda Timberlake

Harrison House
Tulsa, Oklahoma

Unless otherwise indicated, all Scripture quotations are taken from the *King James Version* of the Bible.

Lifesavers: For Your Marriage —
Practical Easy-To-Use Ideas To Strengthen Your Marriage
ISBN 0-89274-795-1

Christian Faith Center
101 S. Peachtree Street
P.O. Box 100
Creedmoor, North Carolina 27522

Published by Harrison House, Inc.
P. O. Box 35035
Tulsa, Oklahoma 74153

Printed in the United States of America.

Introduction

Strengthening your marriage relationship has never been more important than it is today. As a Christian, you must renew your mind with the Word of God to bring about the joy and victory that He intended for you and your loved one. *Lifesavers: For Your Marriage* is a powerful collection of Scriptures and quotes by Mack and Brenda Timberlake that will help you understand God's perfect plan for your marriage.

Full of Godly wisdom and humor, these quotes and verses will strengthen your faith and bring a new and fresh desire to enjoy God's best in your marriage relationship. This book has something for every marriage, no matter how recent or mature. Whether you are happily married or experiencing rocky times, *Lifesavers: For Your Marriage* will encourage you to put God's Word into practice so that you can experience all that God intended marriage to be.

Marriage is a covenant relationship that should be honored and respected by everyone.

Marriage is honorable in all, and the bed undefiled: but whoremongers and adulterers God will judge.
Hebrews 13:4

A marriage in agreement sets miracles in motion.

Again I say unto you, that if two of you shall agree on earth as touching any thing that they shall ask, it shall be done for them of my Father which is in heaven.
Matthew 18:19

Allow God to love your mate through you.

But God commendeth his love toward us, in that, while we were yet sinners, Christ died for us.
Romans 5:8

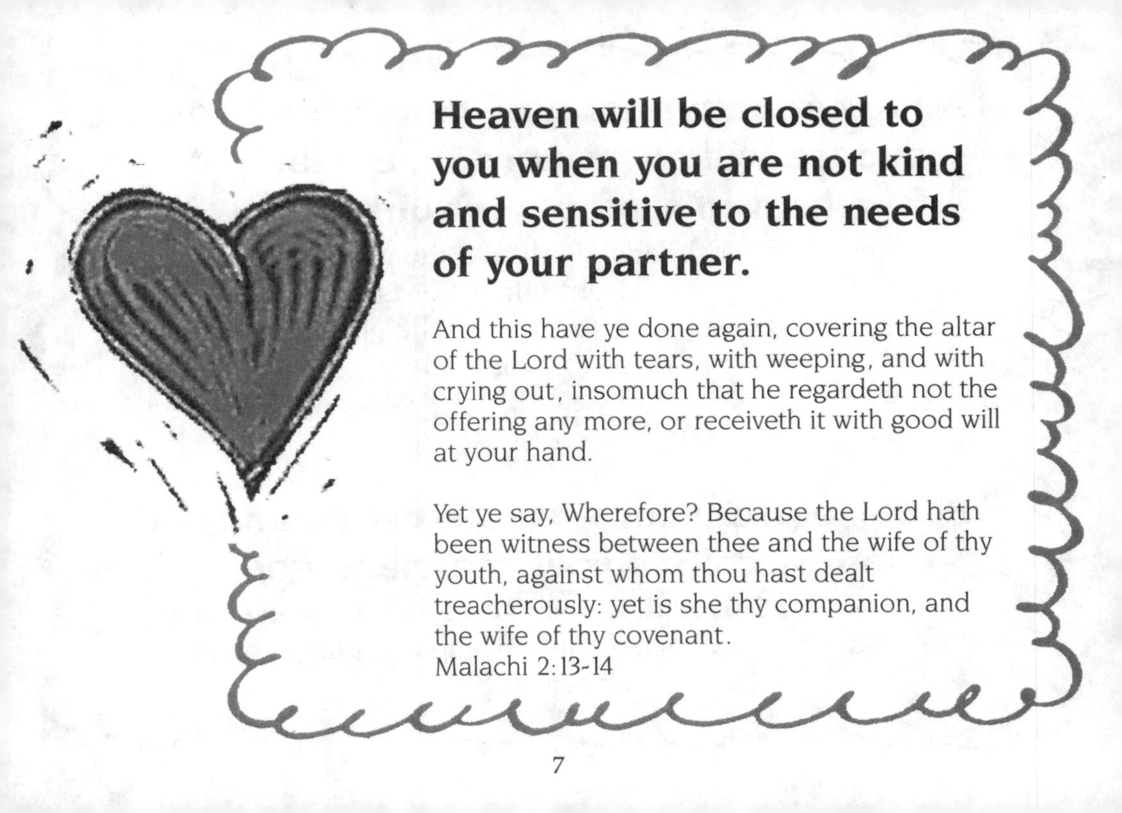

Heaven will be closed to you when you are not kind and sensitive to the needs of your partner.

And this have ye done again, covering the altar of the Lord with tears, with weeping, and with crying out, insomuch that he regardeth not the offering any more, or receiveth it with good will at your hand.

Yet ye say, Wherefore? Because the Lord hath been witness between thee and the wife of thy youth, against whom thou hast dealt treacherously: yet is she thy companion, and the wife of thy covenant.
Malachi 2:13-14

A lack of understanding concerning your spouse will always produce a lack of heaven's supply in your life.

Likewise, ye husbands, dwell with them according to knowledge, giving honour unto the wife, as unto the weaker vessel, and as being heirs together of the grace of life; that your prayers be not hindered.

1 Peter 3:7

Become pregnant with the expectancy of God by calling your marriage good.

And the Lord God said, It is not good that the man should be alone; I will make him an help meet for him.

Genesis 2:18

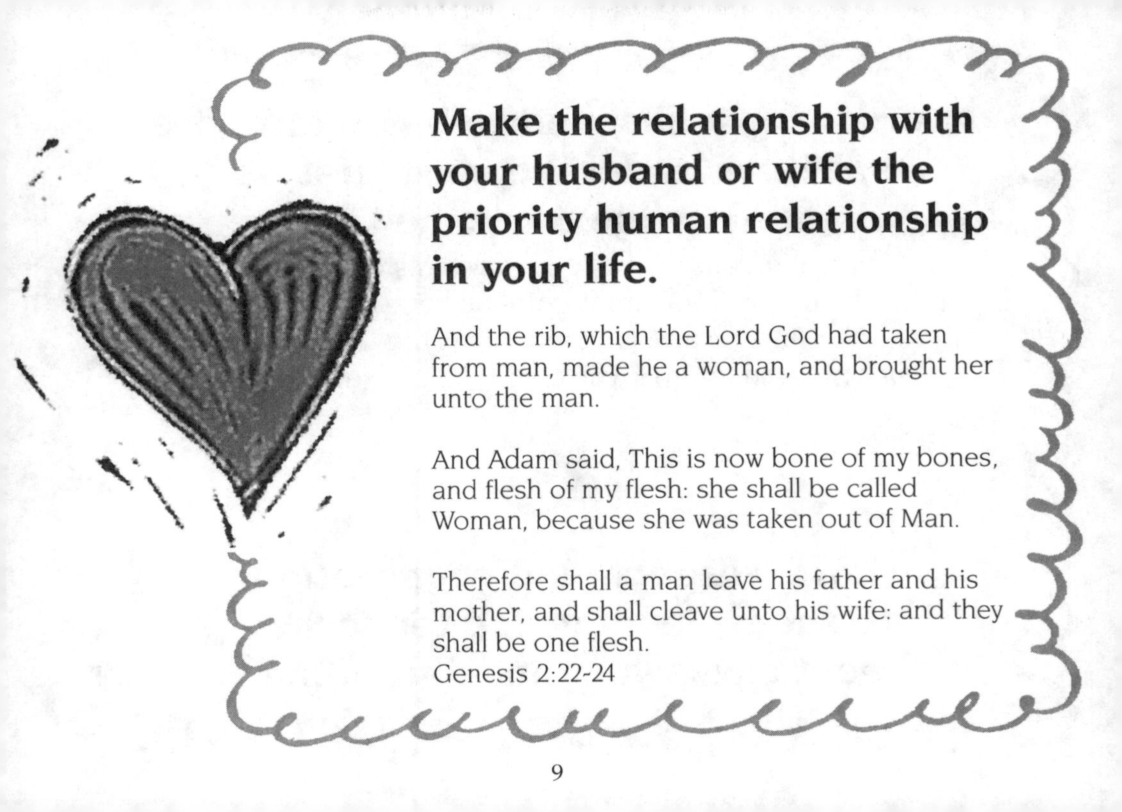

Make the relationship with your husband or wife the priority human relationship in your life.

And the rib, which the Lord God had taken from man, made he a woman, and brought her unto the man.

And Adam said, This is now bone of my bones, and flesh of my flesh: she shall be called Woman, because she was taken out of Man.

Therefore shall a man leave his father and his mother, and shall cleave unto his wife: and they shall be one flesh.
Genesis 2:22-24

In order for a husband to be an effective spiritual leader, he must first be directed by the Supreme Leader.

For I know him, that he will command his children and his household after him, and they shall keep the way of the Lord, to do justice and judgment; that the Lord may bring upon Abraham that which he hath spoken of him.
Genesis 18:19

Love, respect, and cooperation are the fruits of giving tenderness, gentleness, and understanding.

Let the inside of your spiritual house be more beautiful than the outside of your spiritual house.

Know ye not that ye are the temple of God, and that the Spirit of God dwelleth in you?
1 Corinthians 3:16

Be willing and determined to work on your marriage relationship.

Likewise, ye wives, be in subjection to your own husbands; that, if any obey not the word, they also may without the word be won by the conversation of the wives.
1 Peter 3:1

The continual renewal of your love towards your spouse takes place in three areas of your life: 1) Your will; 2) Your actions; and, 3) Your feelings.

Confess your love and commitment to your spouse often. Your confession will close the door to unfaithfulness.

Seeing then that we have a great high priest, that is passed into the heavens, Jesus the Son of God, let us hold fast our profession.
Hebrews 4:14

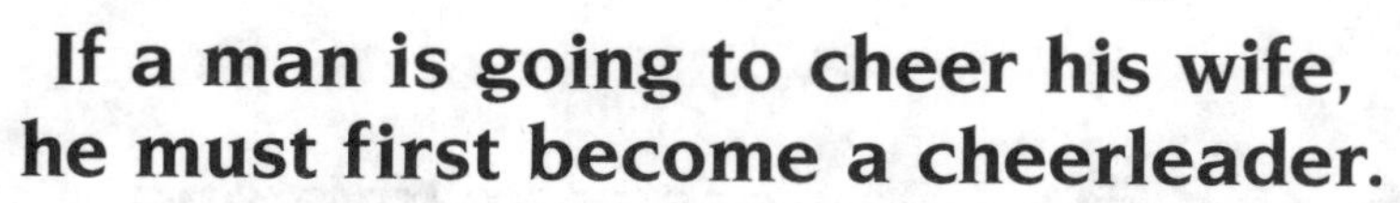

If a man is going to cheer his wife, he must first become a cheerleader.

Her children arise up, and call her blessed;
her husband also, and he praiseth her.
Proverbs 31:28

Don't wait for your spouse to change before you commit to being unselfish.

Greater love hath no man than this,
that a man lay down his life for his friends.
John 15:13

The secret to your mate's heart is to make him or her feel important.

Even as Sara obeyed Abraham, calling him lord: whose daughters ye are, as long as ye do well, and are not afraid with any amazement.
1 Peter 3:6

Divine order in a marriage will produce divine peace.

But I would have you know, that the head of every man is Christ; and the head of the woman is the man; and the head of Christ is God.

1 Corinthians 11:3

It is important to know how to handle disagreements rather than how to win arguments.

A soft answer turneth away wrath: but grievous words stir up anger.

Proverbs 15:1

A man's worth is determined by his contributions and achievements. If he does not know his value in life and to others, he will not esteem your value as a woman.

Then said Elkanah her husband to her, Hannah, why weepest thou? and why eatest thou not? and why is thy heart grieved? am not I better to thee than ten sons?
1 Samuel 1:8

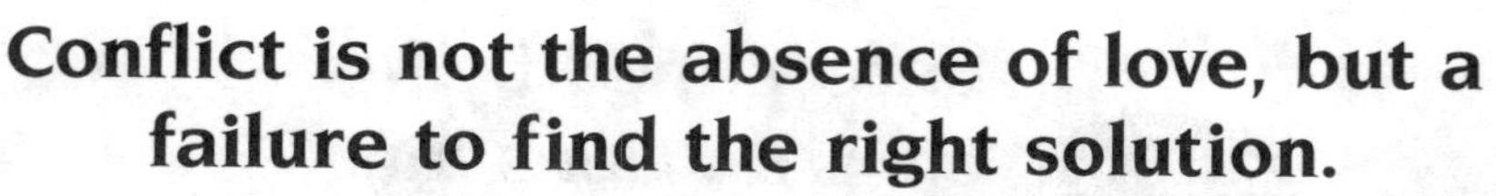

Conflict is not the absence of love, but a failure to find the right solution.

He that handleth a matter wisely shall find good: and whoso trusteth in the Lord, happy is he.
Proverbs 16:20

People who are in love can't wait to touch each other.

A workable solution considers the needs of both partners.

Through wisdom is an house builded; and by understanding it is established:

And by knowledge shall the chambers be filled with all precious and pleasant riches.

A wise man is strong; yea, a man of knowledge increaseth strength.
Proverbs 24:3-5

Don't let role expectations stop you when it comes to helping each other complete a project or a task together.

My little children, let us not love in word, neither in tongue; but in deed and in truth.
1 John 3:8

It is easier to change actions, than to change feelings.

Hereby perceive we the love of God, because he laid down his life for us: and we ought to lay down our lives for the brethren.
1 John 3:16

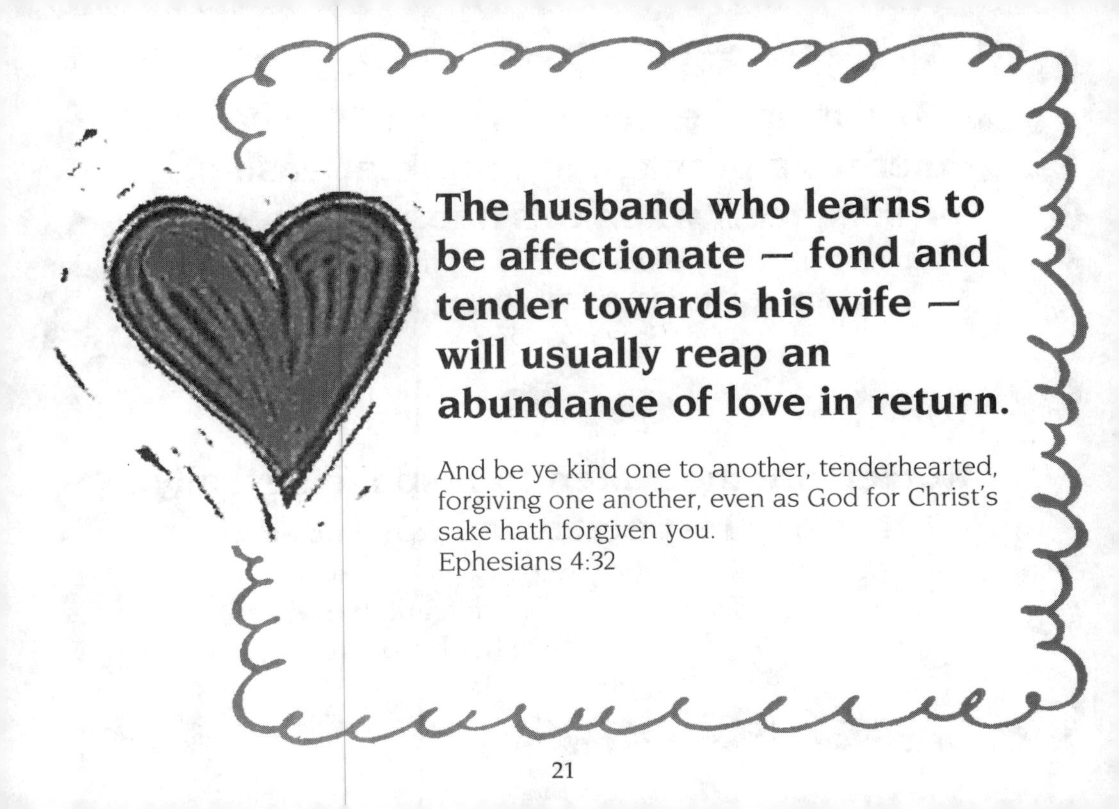

The husband who learns to be affectionate — fond and tender towards his wife — will usually reap an abundance of love in return.

And be ye kind one to another, tenderhearted, forgiving one another, even as God for Christ's sake hath forgiven you.
Ephesians 4:32

Try using the words, "we" or "I" when there is a problem in your relationship. For instance, "When this happens, I feel...."

A man hath joy by the answer of his mouth: and a word spoken in due season, how good is it!
Proverbs 15:23

Women are motivated to respond sexually if they are respected and appreciated.

Nevertheless let every one of you in particular so love his wife even as himself; and the wife see that she reverence her husband.
Ephesians 5:33

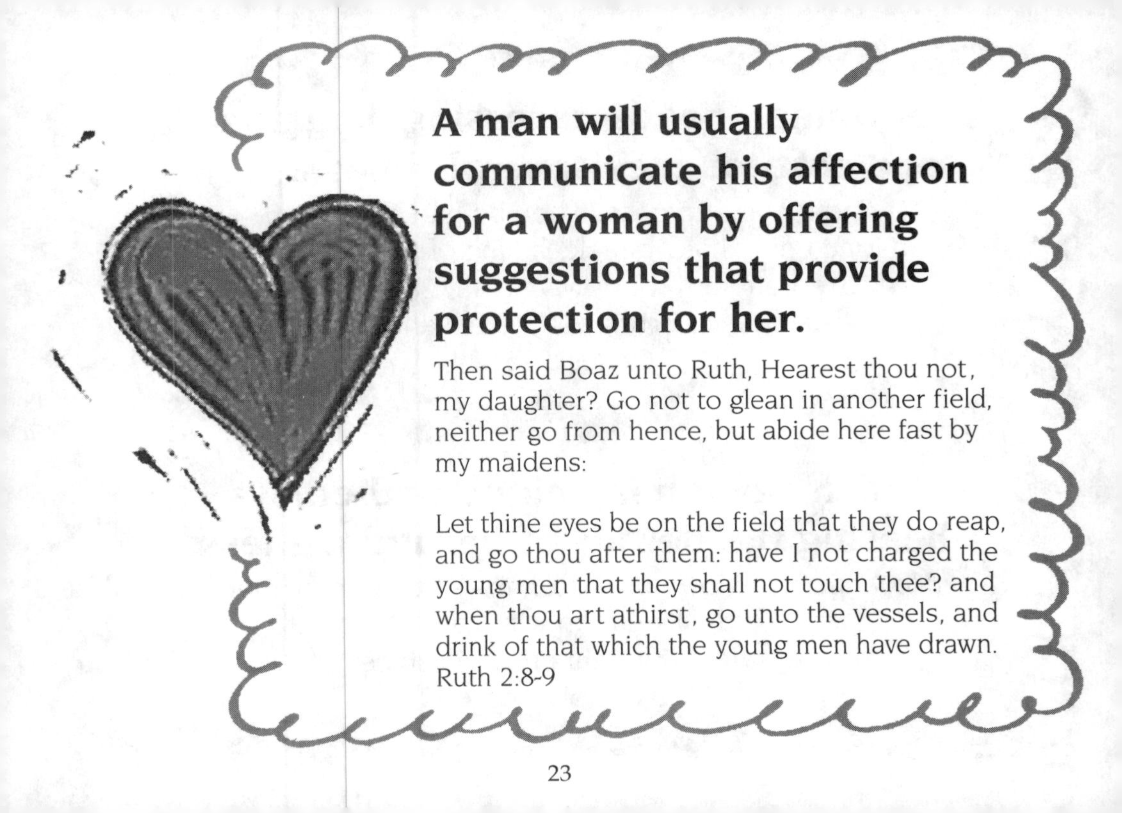

A man will usually communicate his affection for a woman by offering suggestions that provide protection for her.

Then said Boaz unto Ruth, Hearest thou not, my daughter? Go not to glean in another field, neither go from hence, but abide here fast by my maidens:

Let thine eyes be on the field that they do reap, and go thou after them: have I not charged the young men that they shall not touch thee? and when thou art athirst, go unto the vessels, and drink of that which the young men have drawn.
Ruth 2:8-9

A woman needs caressing, hugging, and soft touches several times a day.

And it came to pass, when he had been there a long time, that Abimelech king of the Philistines looked out at a window, and saw, and, behold, Isaac was sporting with Rebekah his wife.
Genesis 26:8

Each woman is unique and enjoys hearing the details of her uniqueness.

How fair is thy love, my sister, my spouse! how much better is thy love than wine! and the smell of thine ointments than all spices!
Song of Solomon 4:10

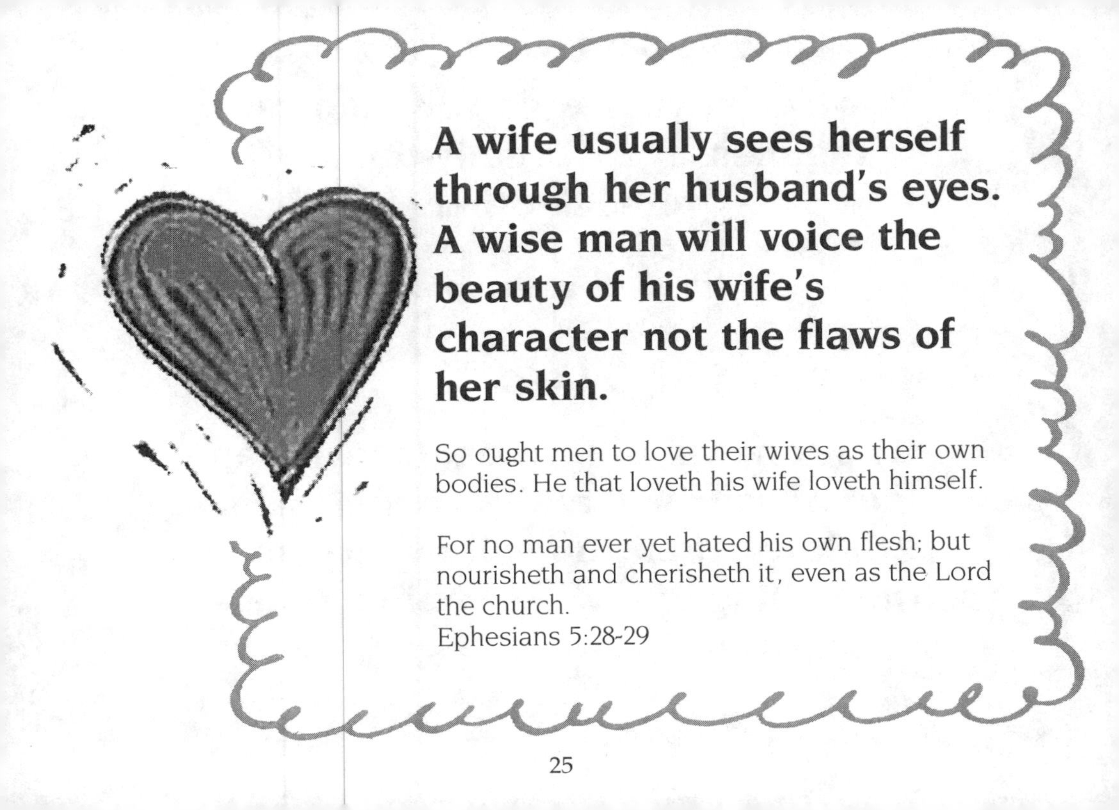

A wife usually sees herself through her husband's eyes. A wise man will voice the beauty of his wife's character not the flaws of her skin.

So ought men to love their wives as their own bodies. He that loveth his wife loveth himself.

For no man ever yet hated his own flesh; but nourisheth and cherisheth it, even as the Lord the church.
Ephesians 5:28-29

Always let your eyes communicate the message, "I really do care" to each other.

Behold, thou art fair, my love; behold, thou art fair; thou hast doves' eyes.
Song of Solomon 1:15

The renewal of love begins with an act of your will and a commitment to love. Then you will experience the feeling of joy — of being in love.

Beloved, if God so loved us, we ought also to love one another.
1 John 4:11

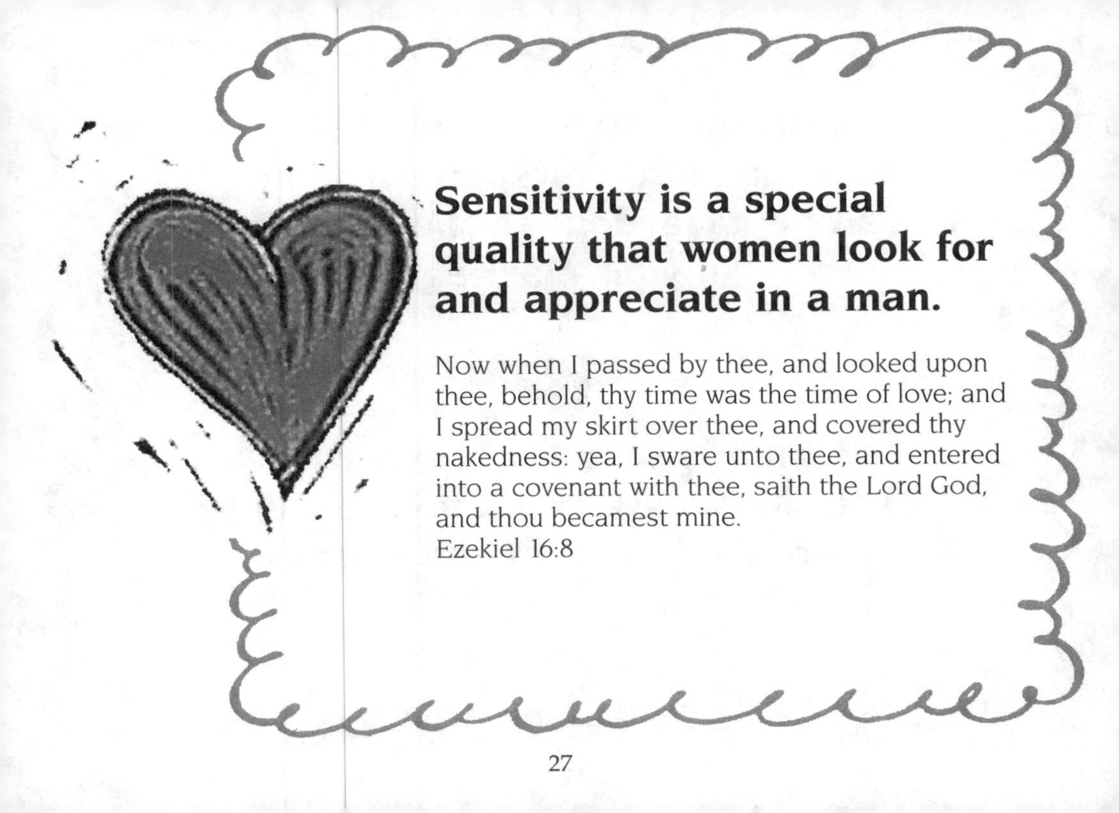

Sensitivity is a special quality that women look for and appreciate in a man.

Now when I passed by thee, and looked upon thee, behold, thy time was the time of love; and I spread my skirt over thee, and covered thy nakedness: yea, I sware unto thee, and entered into a covenant with thee, saith the Lord God, and thou becamest mine.
Ezekiel 16:8

Caution! Too much television watching and newspaper reading can be hazardous to the affection in your marriage.

A man is sexually aroused by what he sees; a woman is sexually aroused by what she hears.

The hearing ear, and the seeing eye,
the Lord hath made even both of them.
Proverbs 20:12

The timing is always perfect for a man to give his wife a gift because she is special to him.

I decked thee also with ornaments, and I put bracelets upon thy hands, and a chain on thy neck.

And I put a jewel on thy forehead, and earrings in thine ears, and a beautiful crown upon thine head.
Ezekiel 16:11-12

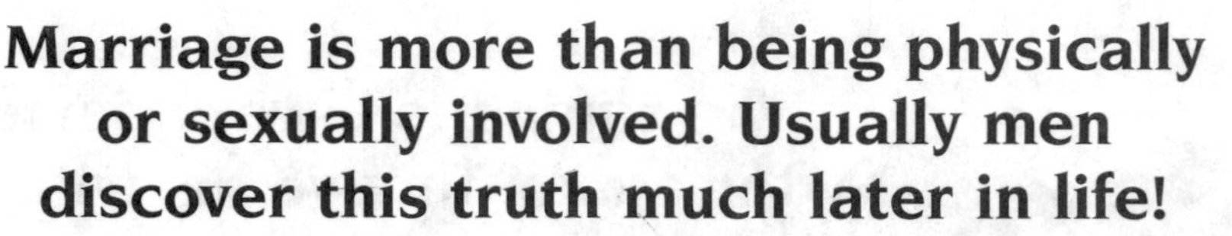

Marriage is more than being physically or sexually involved. Usually men discover this truth much later in life!

Let thy fountain be blessed: and rejoice
with the wife of thy youth.
Proverbs 5:18

In marriage, the "face to face" position is better that the "back to back" position.

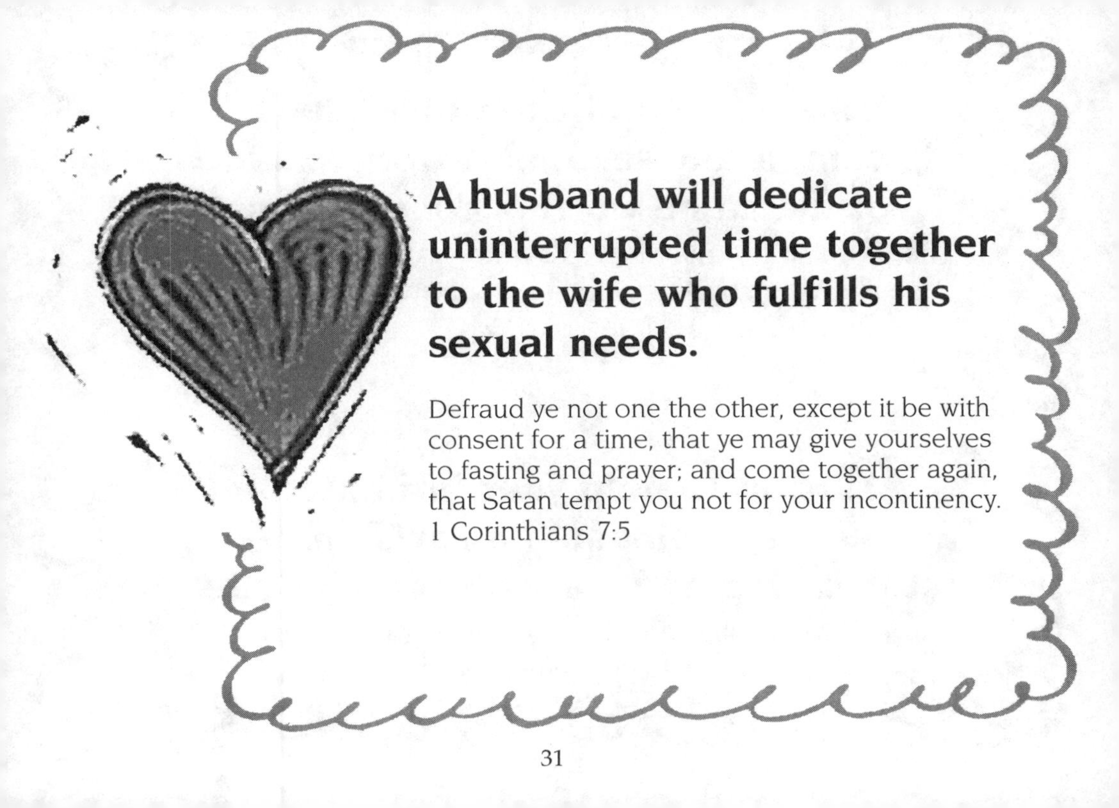

A husband will dedicate uninterrupted time together to the wife who fulfills his sexual needs.

Defraud ye not one the other, except it be with consent for a time, that ye may give yourselves to fasting and prayer; and come together again, that Satan tempt you not for your incontinency.
1 Corinthians 7:5

A man's idea of the word "cleave" is completely sexual. A woman's idea of the same word is commitment.

Therefore shall a man leave his father and his mother, and shall cleave unto his wife: and they shall be one flesh.
Genesis 2:24

Ask God to help your intimate and sexual moments be ravishing — intoxicating and transported by delight.

Live joyfully with the wife whom thou lovest.
Ecclesiastes 9:9a

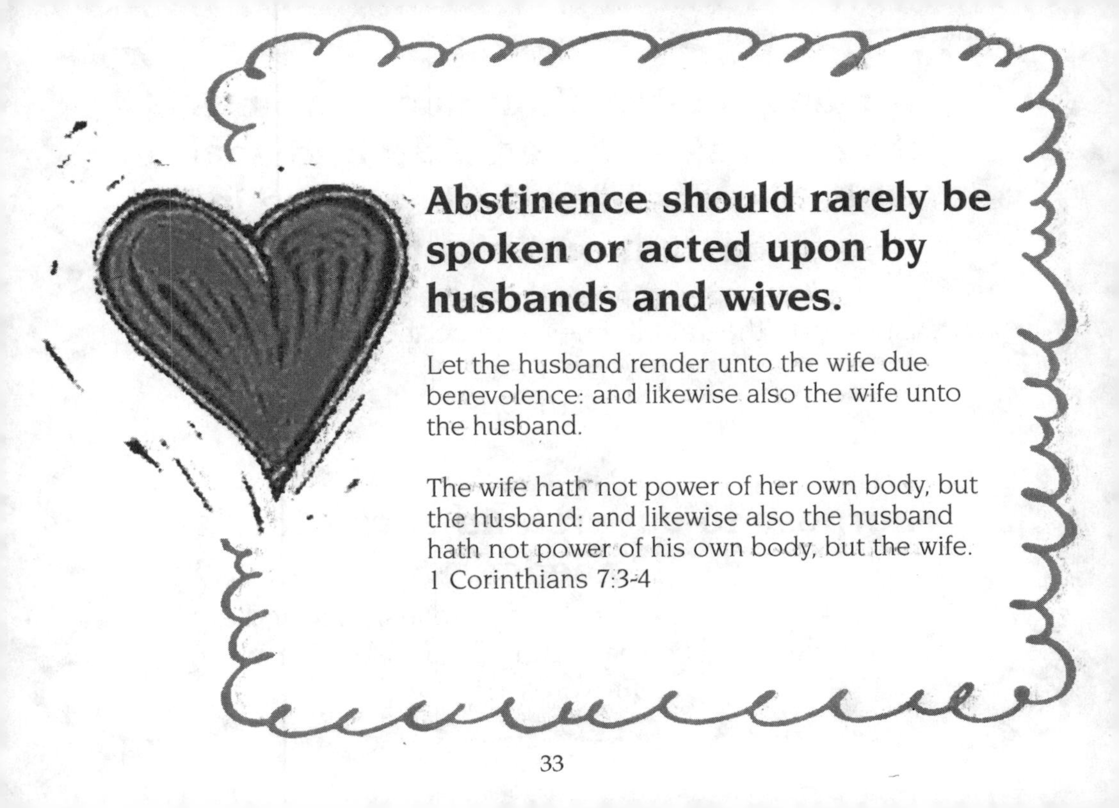

Abstinence should rarely be spoken or acted upon by husbands and wives.

Let the husband render unto the wife due benevolence: and likewise also the wife unto the husband.

The wife hath not power of her own body, but the husband: and likewise also the husband hath not power of his own body, but the wife.
1 Corinthians 7:3-4

A man's feeling of fulfillment comes after he has achieved a desired goal. If he desires his wife, he will be in constant pursuit of her.

Let her be as the loving hind and pleasant roe; let her breasts satisfy thee at all times; and be thou ravished always with her love.
Proverbs 5:19

Purpose to understand each other's needs.

A wise man will hear, and will increase learning; and a man of understanding shall attain unto wise counsels.
Proverbs 1:5

Fantasizing about a person other than your spouse means trouble in the here and now.

Finally, brethren, whatsoever things are true, whatsoever things are honest, whatsoever things are just, whatsoever things are pure, whatsoever things are lovely, whatsoever things are of good report; if there be any virtue, and if there be any praise, think on these things.
Philippians 4:8

Have a knowledge of what pleases your mate.

Happy is the man that findeth wisdom, and the man that getteth understanding.
Proverbs 3:13

These fire-quenchers will kill the spark of romance in a marriage: low self-esteem, depression, anger over hurts of the past, misunderstandings, and fatigue.

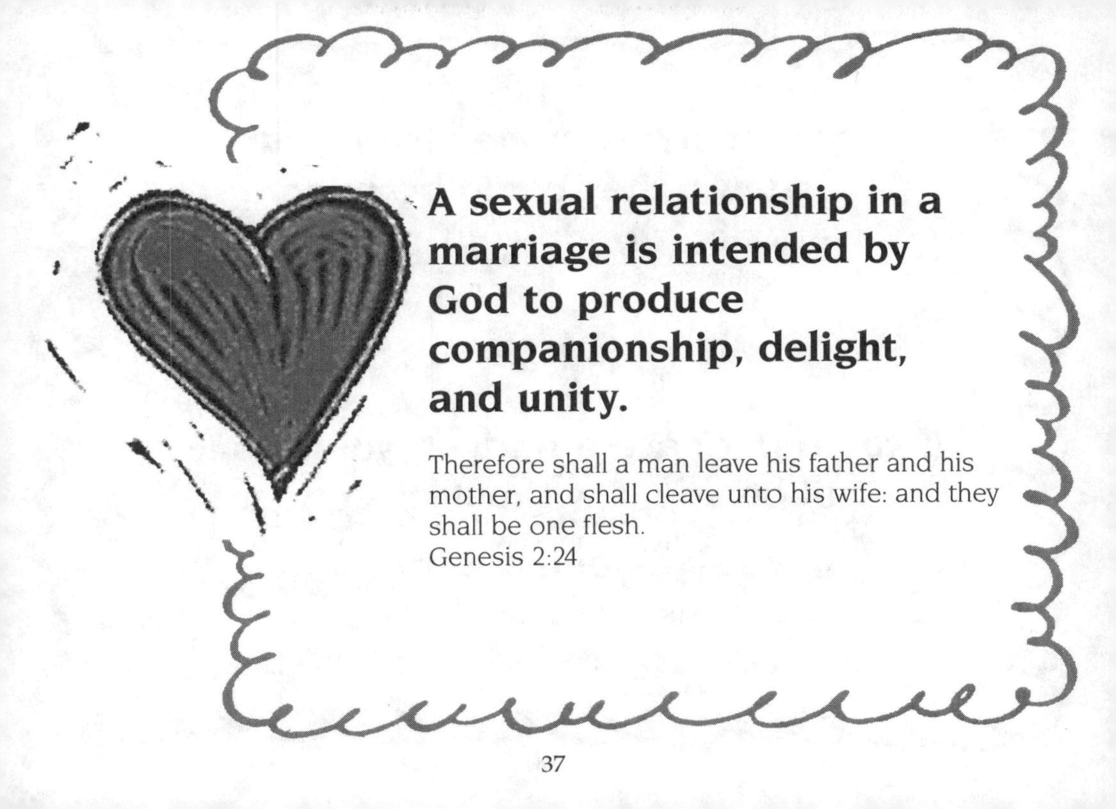

A sexual relationship in a marriage is intended by God to produce companionship, delight, and unity.

Therefore shall a man leave his father and his mother, and shall cleave unto his wife: and they shall be one flesh.
Genesis 2:24

If you borrow money from your in-laws, they could be in on every decision in your marriage.

If you don't have a budget, your money will be spent without direction.

For which of you, intending to build a tower, sitteth not down first, and counteth the cost, whether he have sufficient to finish it?
Luke 14:28

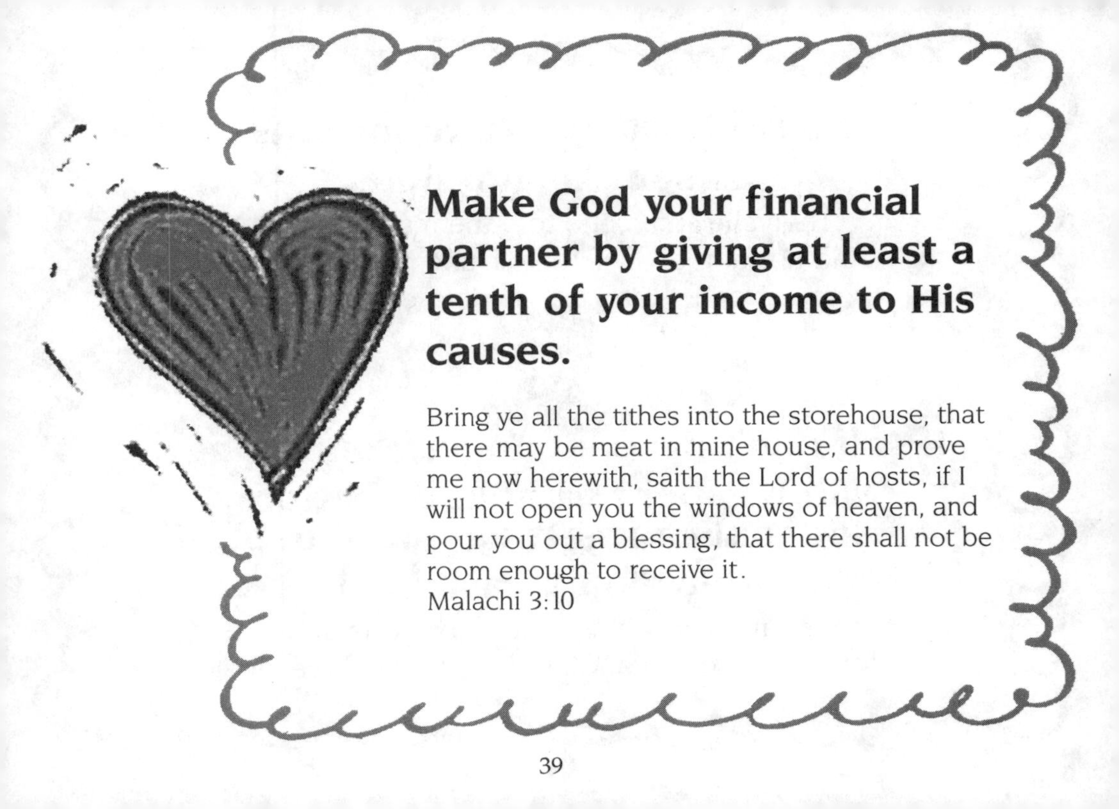

Make God your financial partner by giving at least a tenth of your income to His causes.

Bring ye all the tithes into the storehouse, that there may be meat in mine house, and prove me now herewith, saith the Lord of hosts, if I will not open you the windows of heaven, and pour you out a blessing, that there shall not be room enough to receive it.
Malachi 3:10

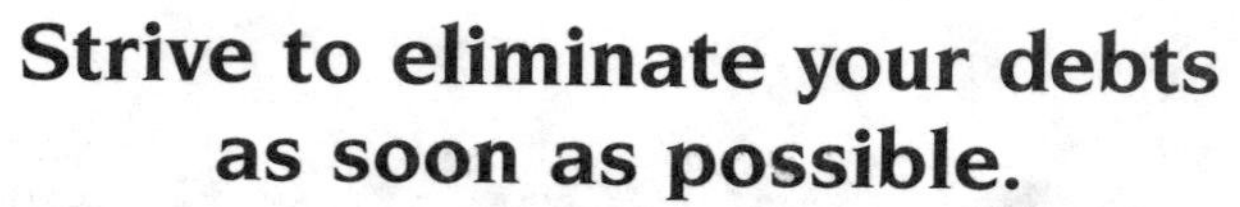

Strive to eliminate your debts as soon as possible.

Then she came and told the man of God.
And he said, Go, sell the oil, and pay thy debt,
and live thou and thy children of the rest.

2 Kings 4:7

Set goals for getting out of debt and live on a cash basis.

Owe no man any thing, but to love one another:
for he that loveth another hath fulfilled the law.

Romans 13:8

Resist impulse buying.

He that hath no rule over his own spirit is like a city that is broken down, and without walls.
Proverbs 25:28

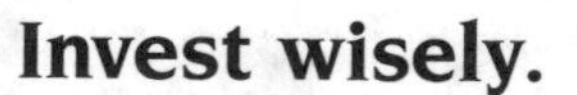

Invest wisely.

The Lord will not suffer the soul of the righteous to famish:
but he casteth away the substance of the wicked.
Proverbs 10:3

**There is a strong need in us all,
to feel loved and not feel used.**

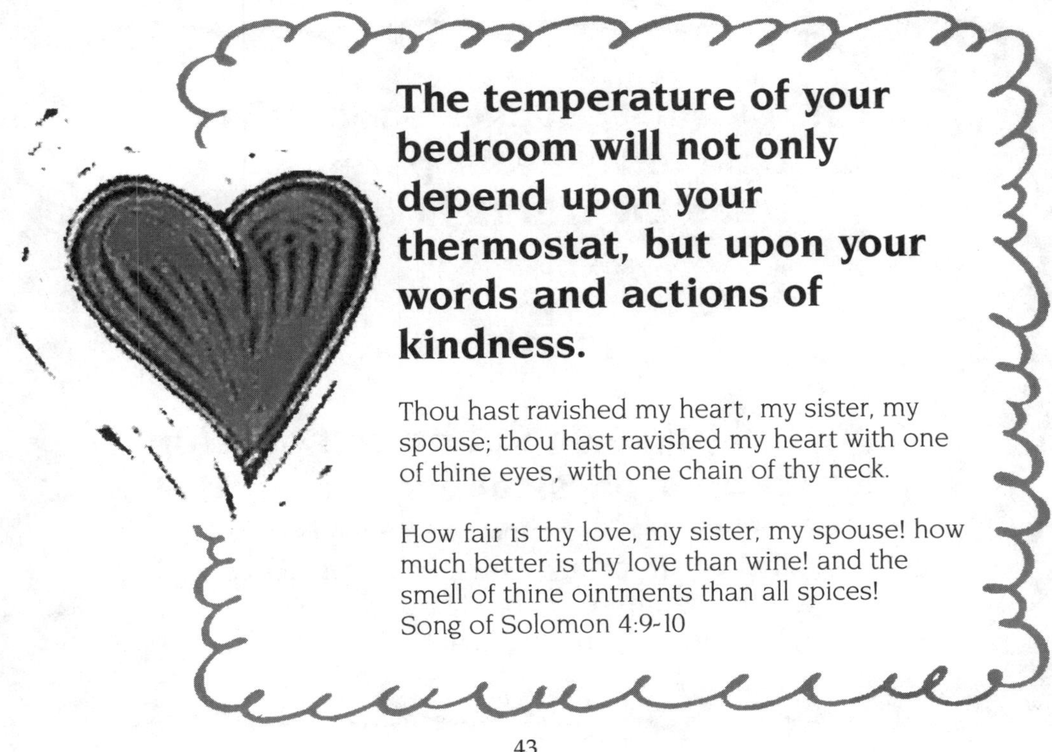

The temperature of your bedroom will not only depend upon your thermostat, but upon your words and actions of kindness.

Thou hast ravished my heart, my sister, my spouse; thou hast ravished my heart with one of thine eyes, with one chain of thy neck.

How fair is thy love, my sister, my spouse! how much better is thy love than wine! and the smell of thine ointments than all spices!
Song of Solomon 4:9-10

If your mate suggests that it is time to visit your parents, plan the trip right away.

A poor physical condition will develop into a poor physical performance.

But I keep under my body, and bring it into subjection: lest that by any means, when I have preached to others, I myself should be a castaway.
1 Corinthians 9:27

The treasure of your spouse's soul will only be discovered when you spend time together in a quite and solitary place.

A time to rend, and a time to sew; a time to keep silence, and a time to speak.
Ecclesiastes 3:7

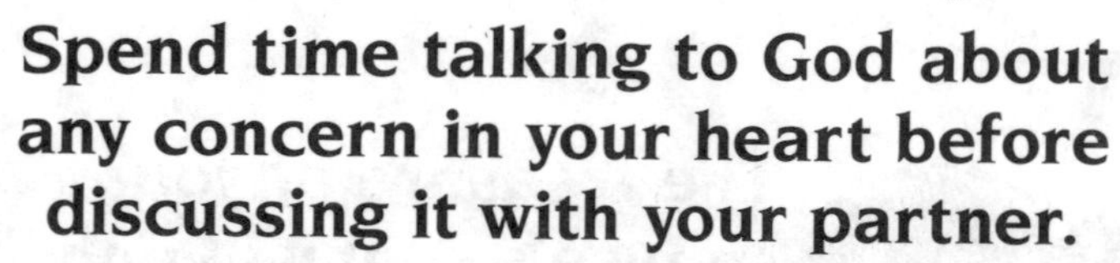

Spend time talking to God about any concern in your heart before discussing it with your partner.

And in the morning, rising up a great while before day, he went out, and departed into a solitary place, and there prayed.
Mark 1:35

If you talk to each other on the run, you are dropping your words on the floor not in the heart and ear of the other.

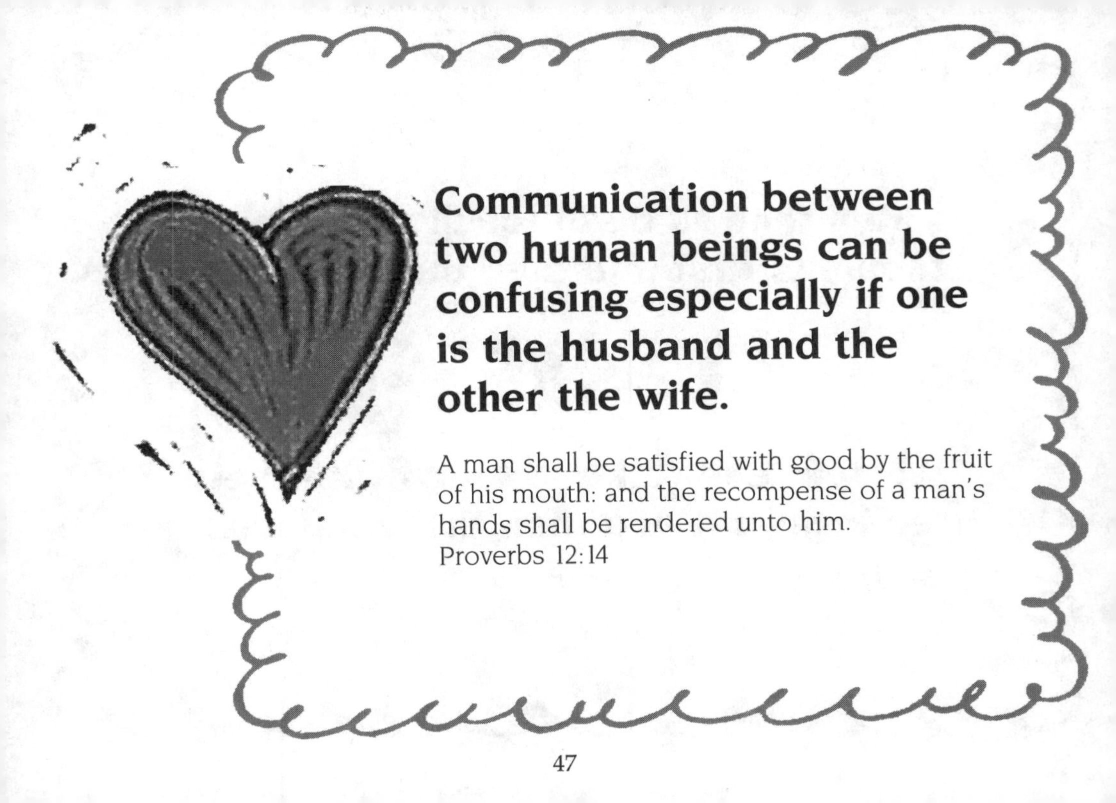

Communication between two human beings can be confusing especially if one is the husband and the other the wife.

A man shall be satisfied with good by the fruit of his mouth: and the recompense of a man's hands shall be rendered unto him.
Proverbs 12:14

Men tend to be in touch with their thoughts first and then their feelings.

Women tend to be in touch with their feelings first and then their thoughts.

The husband who believes himself to be a general on his job, will not talk in generalities to his wife.

A man shall be commended according to his wisdom.
Proverbs 12:8a

Lying to your partner will eventually produce a harvest of mistrust.

A lying tongue hateth those that are afflicted by it;
and a flattering mouth worketh ruin.
Proverbs 26:28

If you are slow to anger, peace is sure to come.

He that is slow to wrath is of great understanding:
but he that is hasty of spirit exalteth folly.
Proverbs 14:29

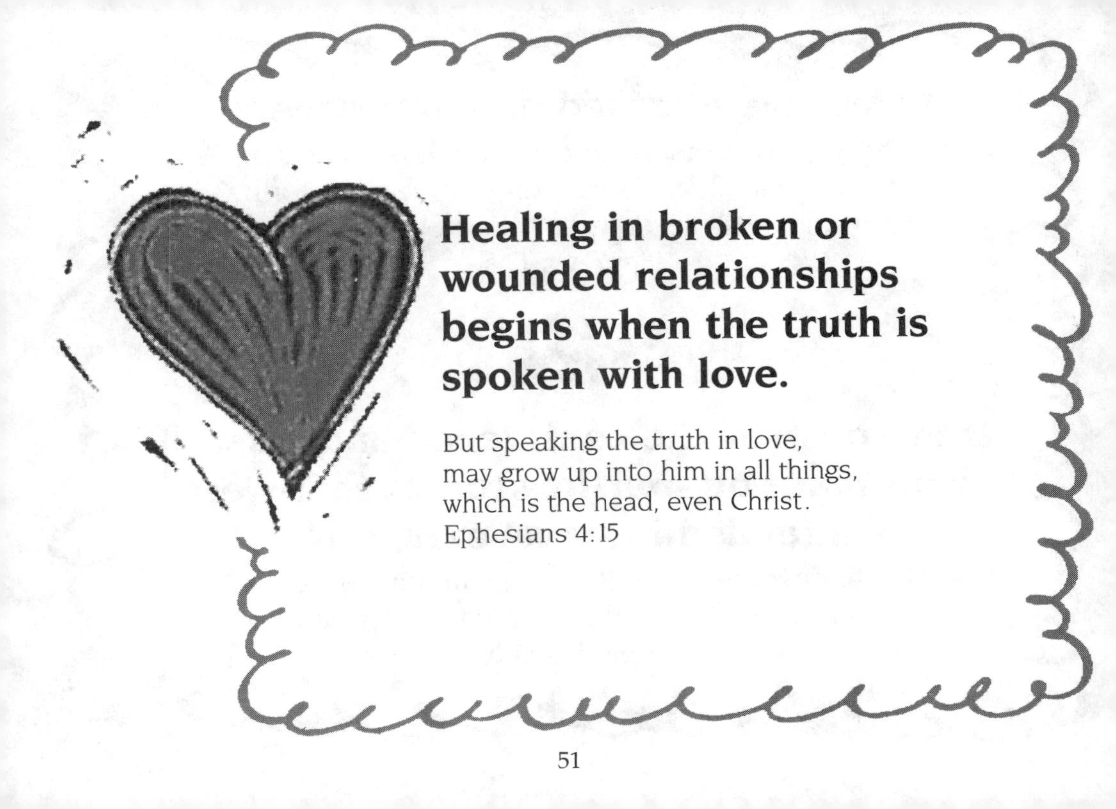

Healing in broken or wounded relationships begins when the truth is spoken with love.

But speaking the truth in love,
may grow up into him in all things,
which is the head, even Christ.
Ephesians 4:15

True love is based on commitment.

Let your conversation be without covetousness;
and be content with such things as ye have: for he
hath said, I will never leave thee, nor forsake thee.
Hebrews 13:5

Don't destroy the confidence and trust of your mate by sharing secrets that were intended for your ears only.

Confidence in an unfaithful man in time of trouble
is like a broken tooth, and a foot out of joint.
Proverbs 25:19

Smile if your spouse has opposite habits and traits from you. God loves diversity.

I will praise thee; for I am fearfully and wonderfully made: marvellous are thy works; and that my soul knoweth right well.
Psalm 139:14

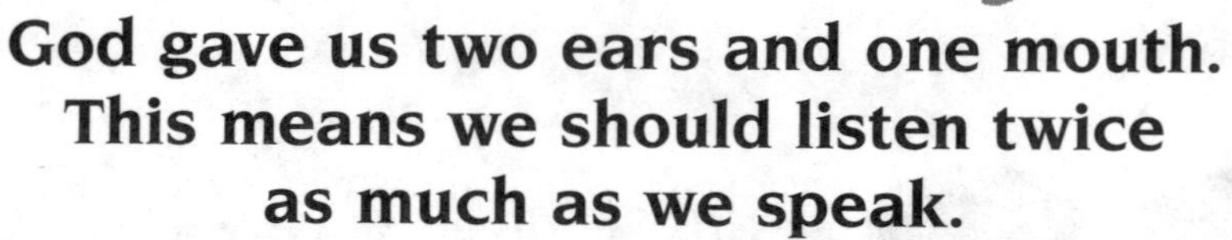

**God gave us two ears and one mouth.
This means we should listen twice
as much as we speak.**

He that answereth a matter before he heareth it,
it is folly and shame unto him.
Proverbs 18:13

**Listening takes a lot of effort, patience,
and sensitivity in a marriage.**

Wherefore, my beloved brethren, let every man
be swift to hear, slow to speak, slow to wrath.
James 1:19

When the person you love is too tired to listen, try using words that will edify and build up.

Let no corrupt communication proceed out of your mouth, but that which is good to the use of edifying, that it may minister grace unto the hearers.
Ephesians 4:29

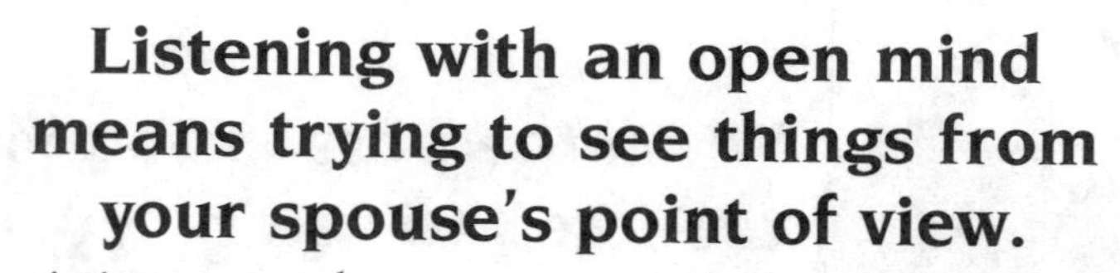

Listening with an open mind means trying to see things from your spouse's point of view.

Submitting yourselves one to another in the fear of God.
Ephesians 5:21

Couples who can't talk about their present problems are headed for bigger problems in the future.

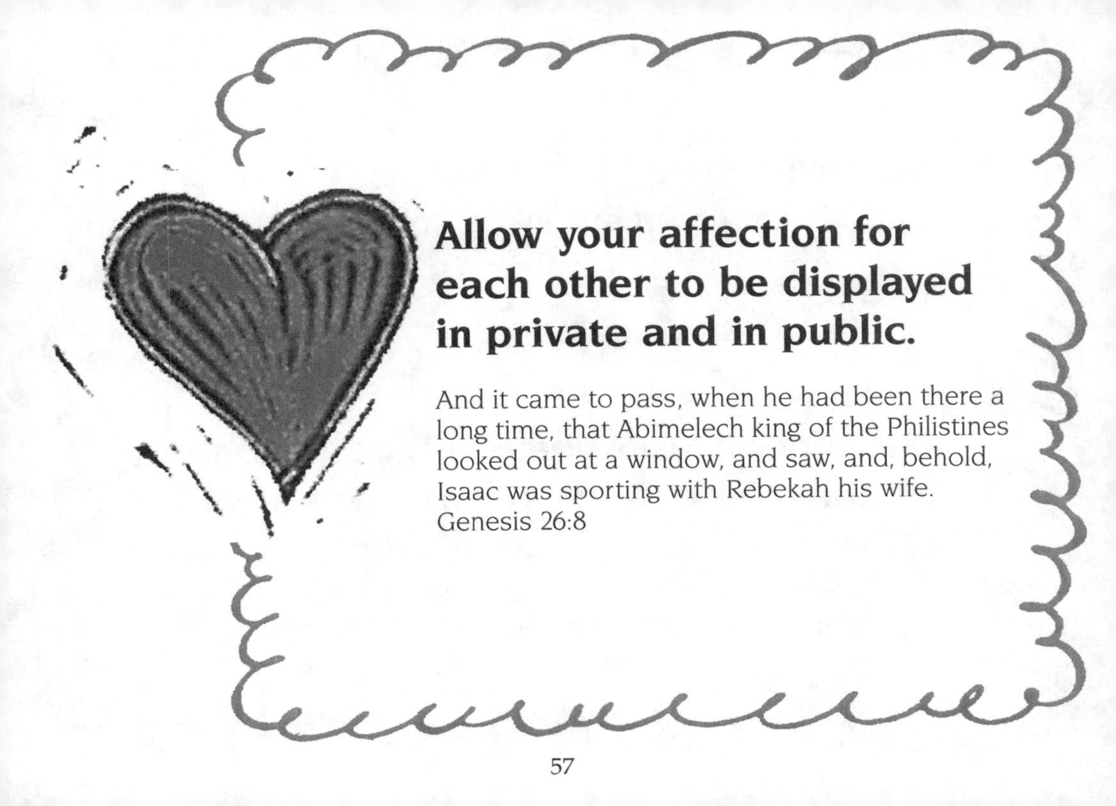

Allow your affection for each other to be displayed in private and in public.

And it came to pass, when he had been there a long time, that Abimelech king of the Philistines looked out at a window, and saw, and, behold, Isaac was sporting with Rebekah his wife.
Genesis 26:8

The *way* you say something is often as important as *what* you say.

The tone of your voice will determine whether the content of your words will gain entry into the ear of the listener.

Let all your things be done with charity.
1 Corinthians 16:14

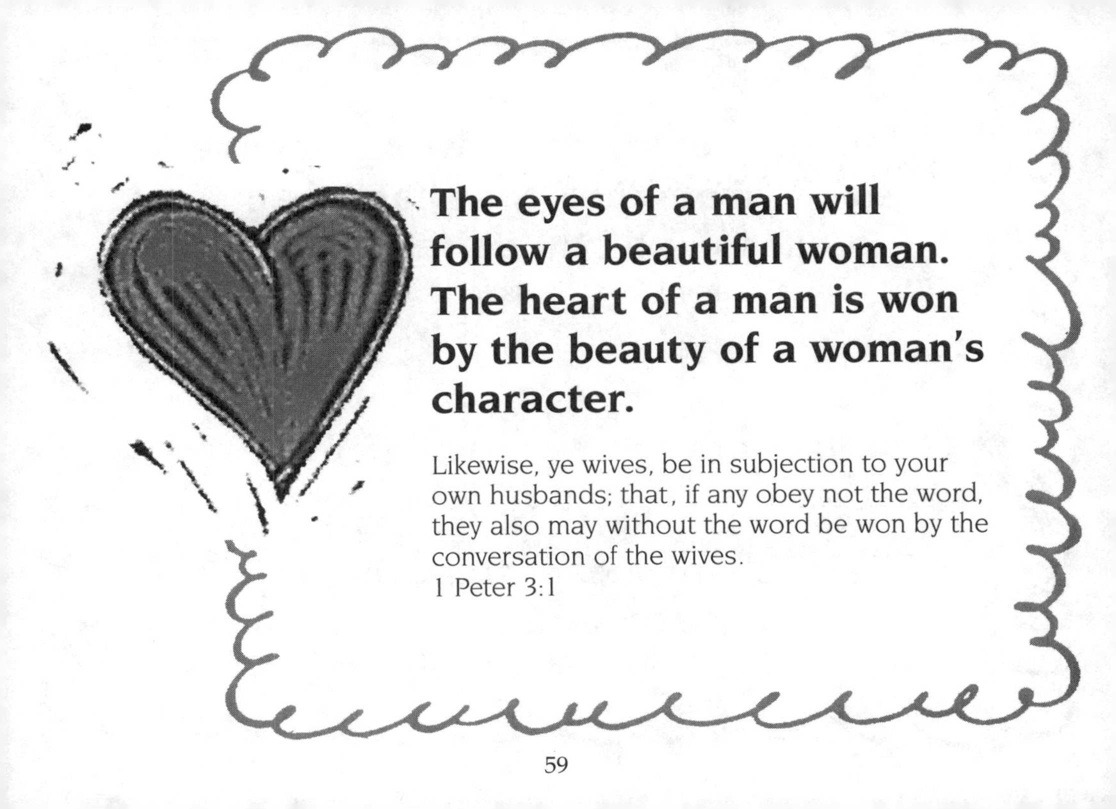

The eyes of a man will follow a beautiful woman. The heart of a man is won by the beauty of a woman's character.

Likewise, ye wives, be in subjection to your own husbands; that, if any obey not the word, they also may without the word be won by the conversation of the wives.
1 Peter 3:1

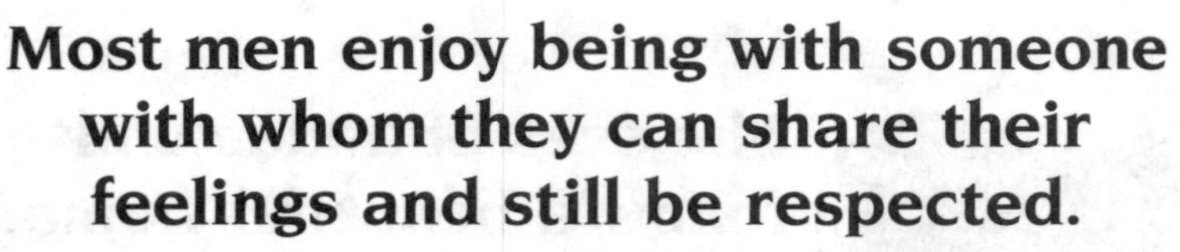

Most men enjoy being with someone with whom they can share their feelings and still be respected.

...and a prudent wife is from the Lord.
Proverbs 19:14b

For a man, setting the romantic stage may mean preparing for an outdoor adventure.

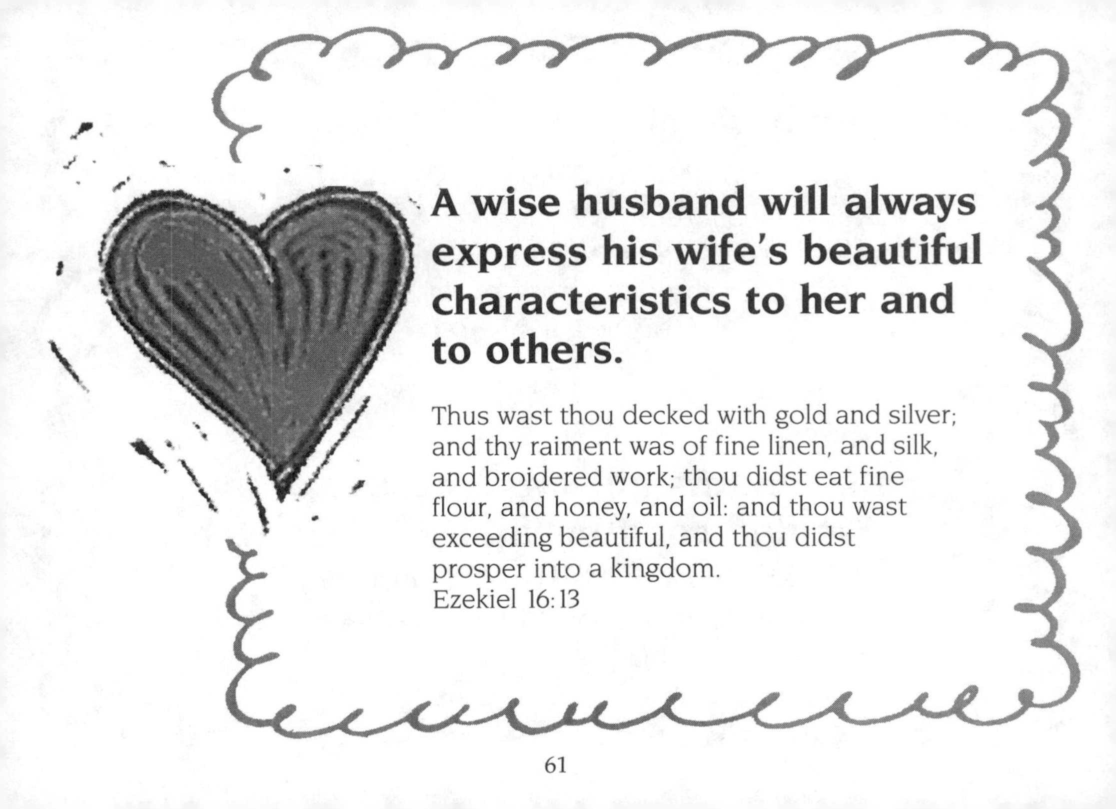

A wise husband will always express his wife's beautiful characteristics to her and to others.

Thus wast thou decked with gold and silver; and thy raiment was of fine linen, and silk, and broidered work; thou didst eat fine flour, and honey, and oil: and thou wast exceeding beautiful, and thou didst prosper into a kingdom.
Ezekiel 16:13

Men enjoy women who hold them in high esteem and respect.

Nevertheless let every one of you in particular
so love his wife even as himself; and the wife see
that she reverence her husband.
Ephesians 5:33

The strengths and weaknesses of men and women counterbalance each other.

Two are better than one; because they
have a good reward for their labour.
Ecclesiastes 4:9

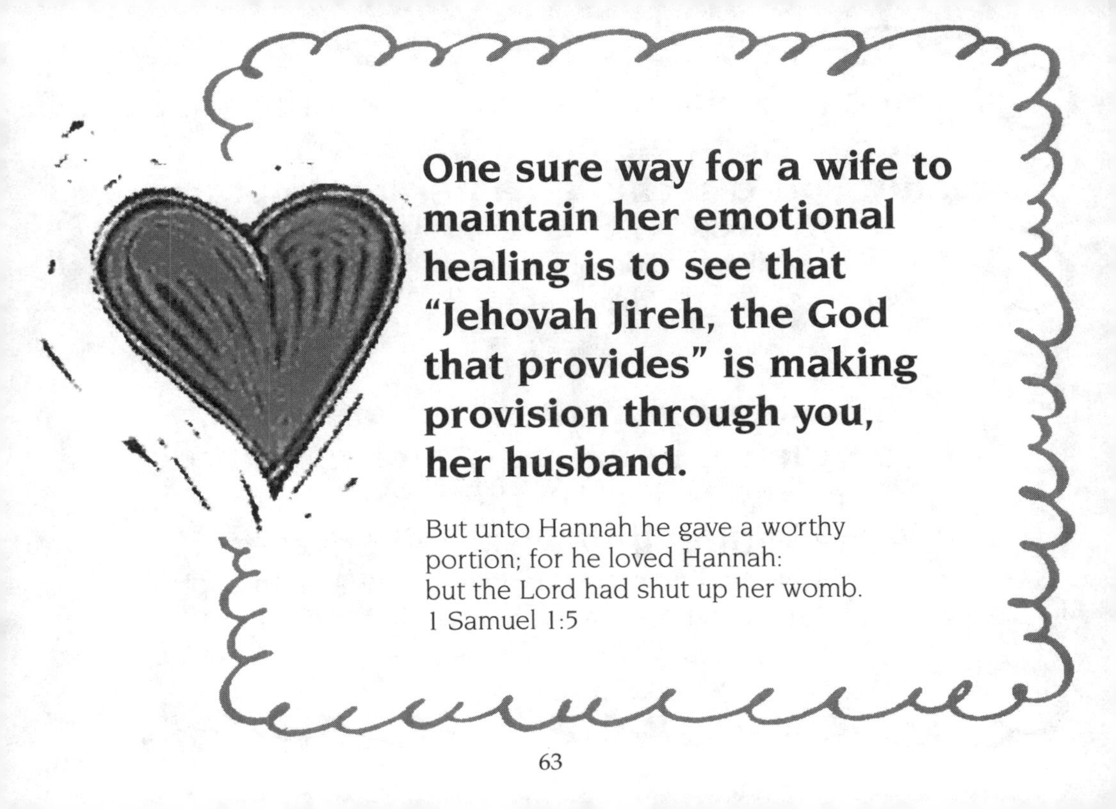

One sure way for a wife to maintain her emotional healing is to see that "Jehovah Jireh, the God that provides" is making provision through you, her husband.

But unto Hannah he gave a worthy portion; for he loved Hannah:
but the Lord had shut up her womb.
1 Samuel 1:5

You can be instrumental in helping your partner change his or her habits. But only God can change a person's nature.

For it is God which worketh in you both to will and to do of his good pleasure.

Philippians 2:13

A husband may demonstrate great confidence in his daily affairs, but a virtuous wife knows the importance of surrounding him with daily prayers.

Praying always with all prayer and supplication in the Spirit, and watching thereunto with all perseverance and supplication for all saints.

Ephesians 6:18

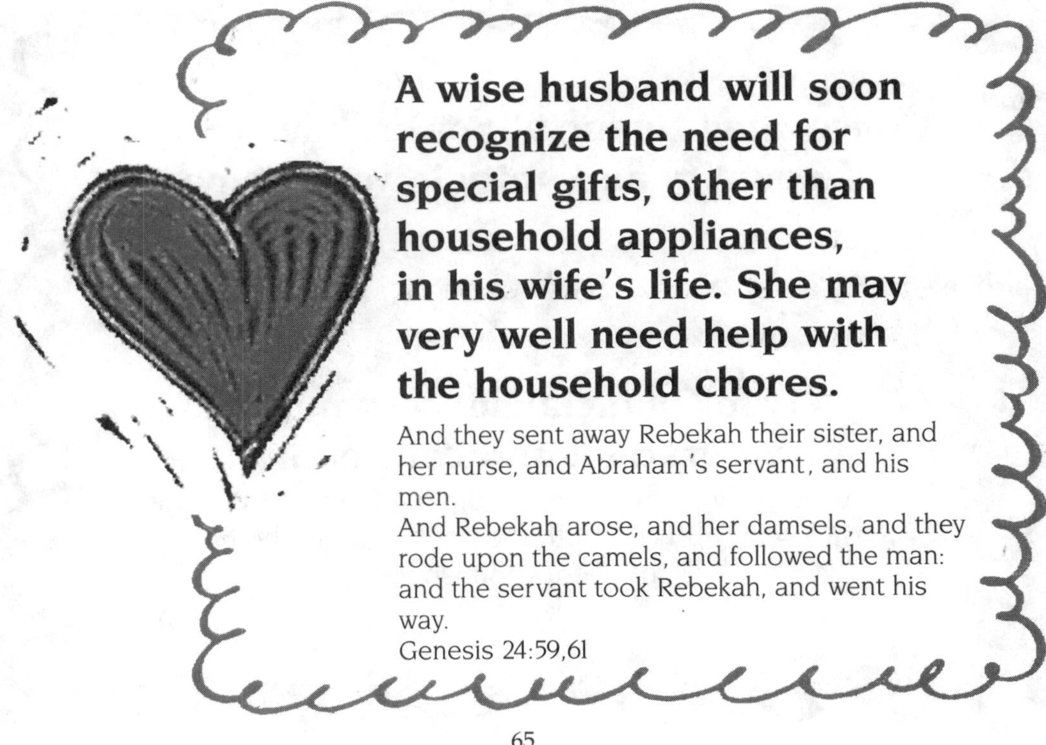

A wise husband will soon recognize the need for special gifts, other than household appliances, in his wife's life. She may very well need help with the household chores.

And they sent away Rebekah their sister, and her nurse, and Abraham's servant, and his men.
And Rebekah arose, and her damsels, and they rode upon the camels, and followed the man: and the servant took Rebekah, and went his way.
Genesis 24:59,61

Concerning financial power, have a goal of equality and unity in your home.

True financial success must be gradual and continual.

For which of you, intending to build a tower, sitteth not down first, and counteth the cost, whether he have sufficient to finish it?
Luke 14:28

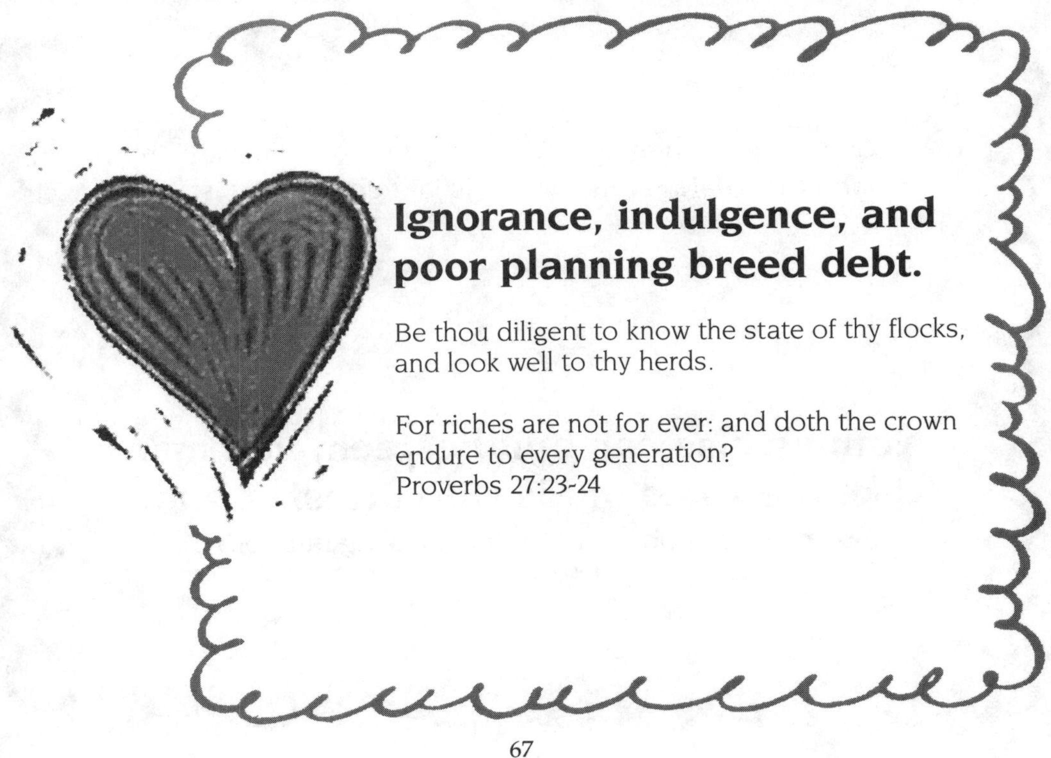

Ignorance, indulgence, and poor planning breed debt.

Be thou diligent to know the state of thy flocks, and look well to thy herds.

For riches are not for ever: and doth the crown endure to every generation?
Proverbs 27:23-24

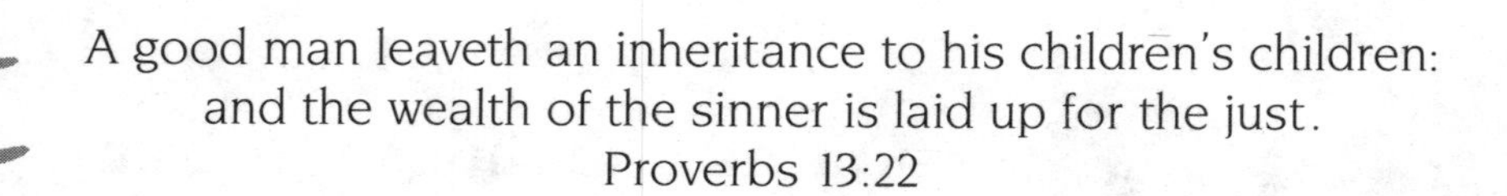

A good man leaveth an inheritance to his children's children:
and the wealth of the sinner is laid up for the just.
Proverbs 13:22

Nothing else can build esteem in a man like the voice of his wife praising him.

Even as Sara obeyed Abraham, calling him lord....
1 Peter 3:6a

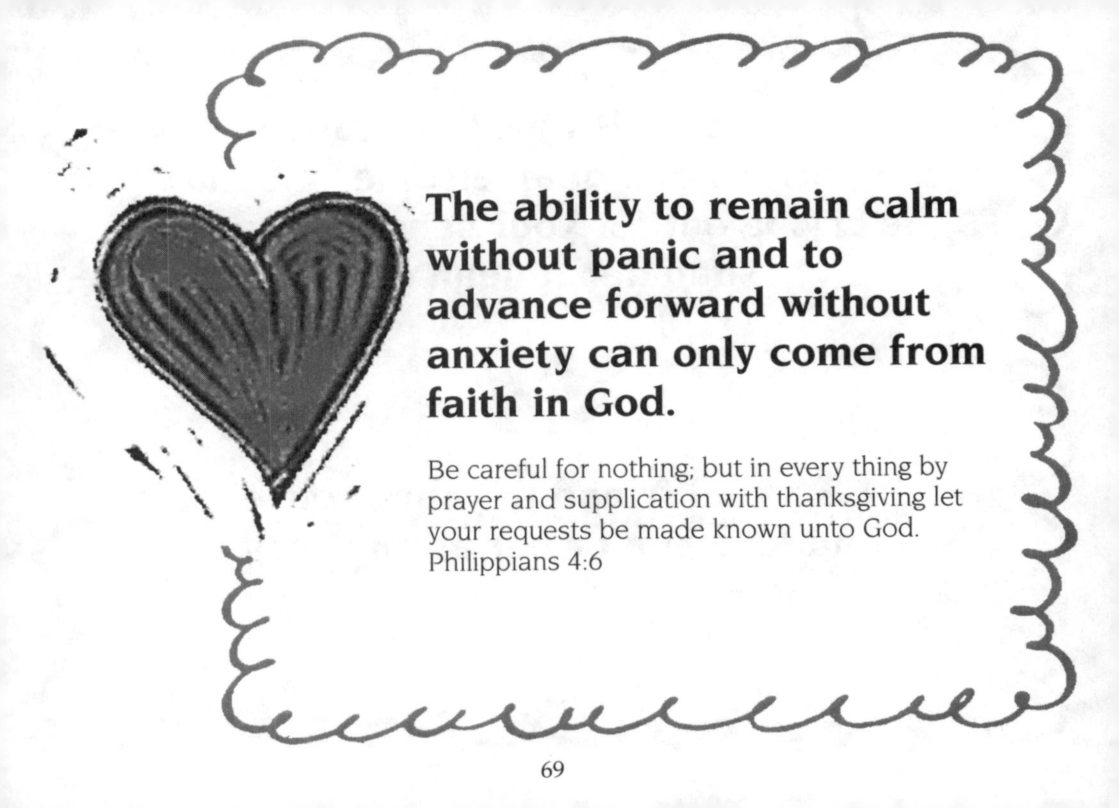

The ability to remain calm without panic and to advance forward without anxiety can only come from faith in God.

Be careful for nothing; but in every thing by prayer and supplication with thanksgiving let your requests be made known unto God.
Philippians 4:6

If your wife is always negative, contentious and quarrelsome, she may be crying out for your sensitivity and shoulder to lean on.

Be a real friend to your spouse and love him or her at all times.

A friend loveth at all times,
and a brother is born for adversity.
Proverbs 17:17

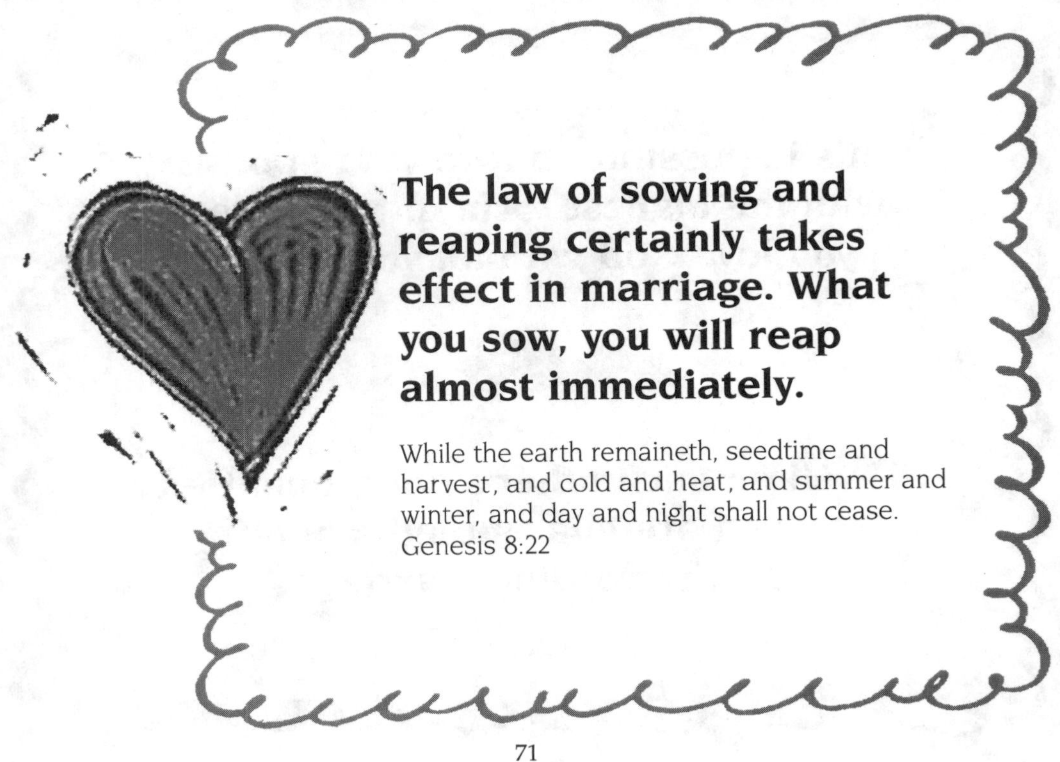

The law of sowing and reaping certainly takes effect in marriage. What you sow, you will reap almost immediately.

While the earth remaineth, seedtime and harvest, and cold and heat, and summer and winter, and day and night shall not cease.
Genesis 8:22

It's impossible to love your spouse with the highest form of love unless you love God with all your heart.

Dwell on each other's good qualities and you are guaranteed a healthy and rewarding marriage.

A husband will return home from work on time each day if his wife remains appealing and attractive.

And it came to pass, when he was come near to enter into Egypt, that he said unto Sarai his wife, Behold now, I know that thou art a fair woman to look upon.
Genesis 12:11

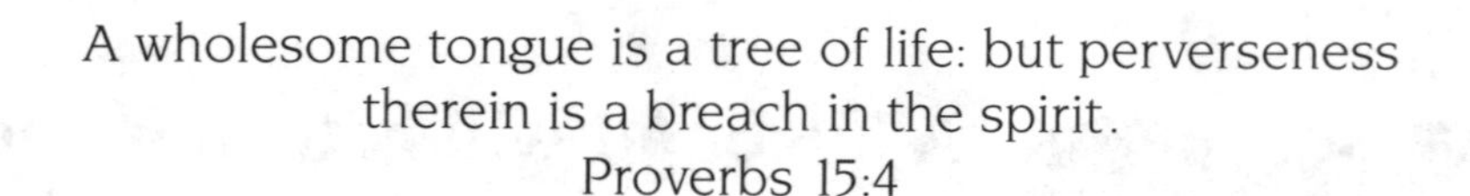

A wholesome tongue is a tree of life: but perverseness therein is a breach in the spirit.
Proverbs 15:4

A merry heart doeth good like a medicine. Try taking extra doses throughout the day.

A merry heart doeth good like a medicine: but a broken spirit drieth the bones.
Proverbs 17:22

Rekindle the flame in your relationship by planning time away together, allowing a budget for this special occasion, and writing it on your calendar.

I am my beloved's, and his desire is toward me.

Come, my beloved, let us go forth into the field; let us lodge in the villages.

Let us get up early to the vineyards; let us see if the vine flourish, whether the tender grape appear, and the pomegranates bud forth: there will I give thee my loves.
Song of Solomon 7:10-12

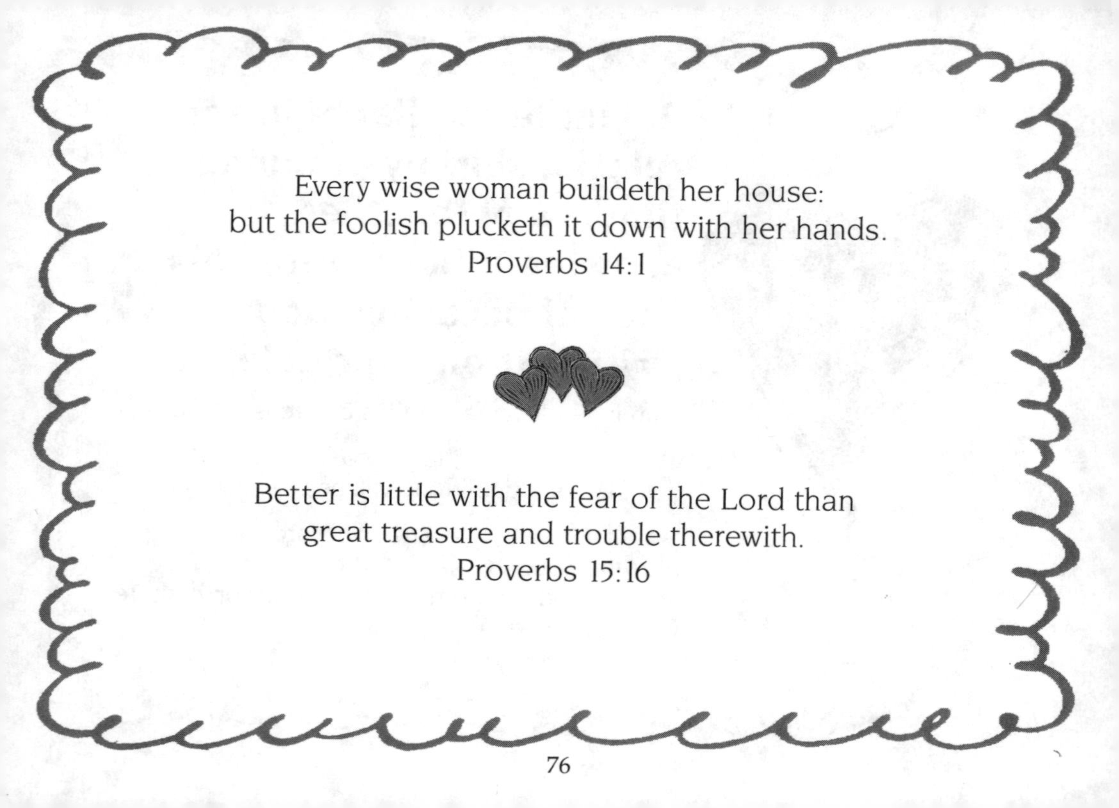

Every wise woman buildeth her house:
but the foolish plucketh it down with her hands.
Proverbs 14:1

Better is little with the fear of the Lord than
great treasure and trouble therewith.
Proverbs 15:16

Great expectations with limited training in the marriage relationship will produce disappointment.

My people are destroyed for lack of knowledge: because thou hast rejected knowledge, I will also reject thee, that thou shalt be no priest to me: seeing thou hast forgotten the law of thy God, I will also forget thy children.
Hosea 4:6

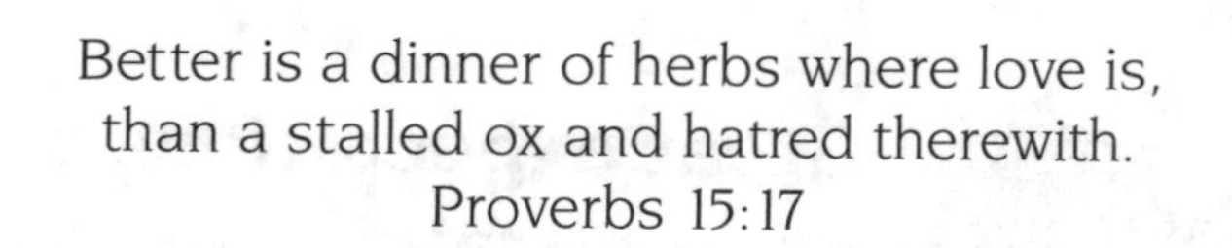

Better is a dinner of herbs where love is,
than a stalled ox and hatred therewith.
Proverbs 15:17

A heavenly atmosphere will appear when agreement in marriage is achieved.

Can two walk together, except they be agreed?
Amos 3:3

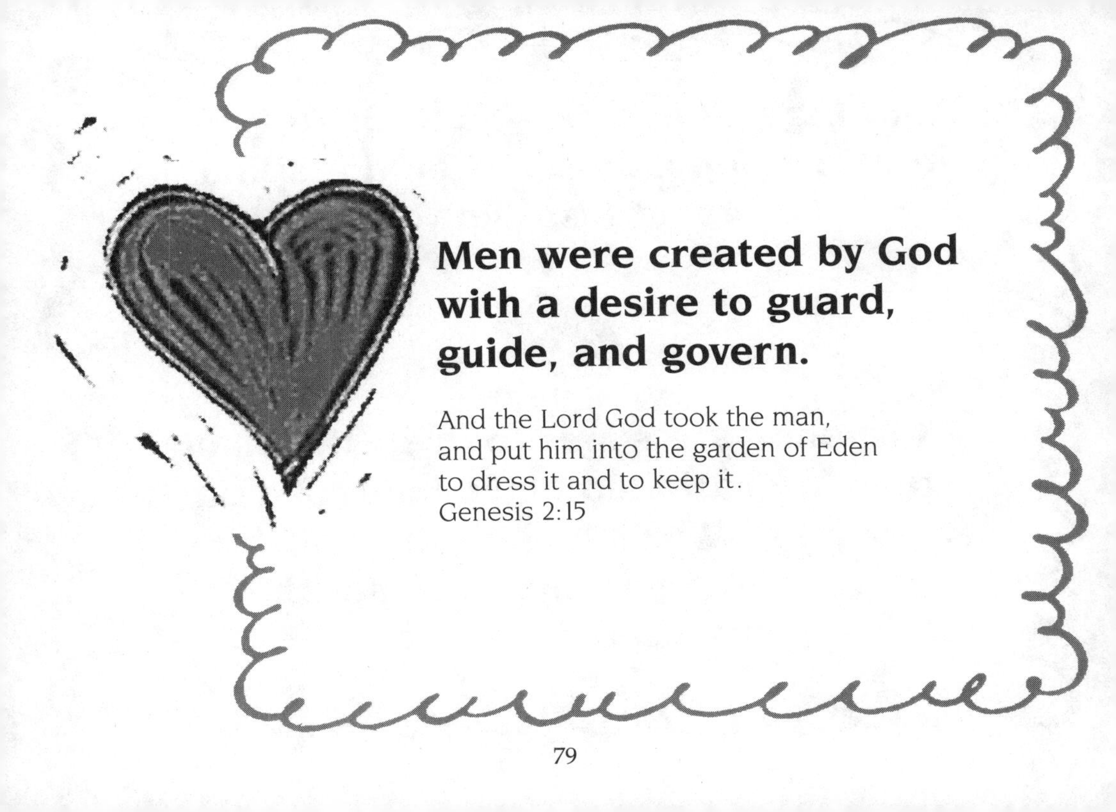

Men were created by God with a desire to guard, guide, and govern.

And the Lord God took the man,
and put him into the garden of Eden
to dress it and to keep it.
Genesis 2:15

Your biggest mistake could be to think that the opposite sex should respond and react just like you do.

Husbands are super to live with when they are satisfied and productive on their jobs. Wives, this is an opportune time to remind them of what they promised to buy you!

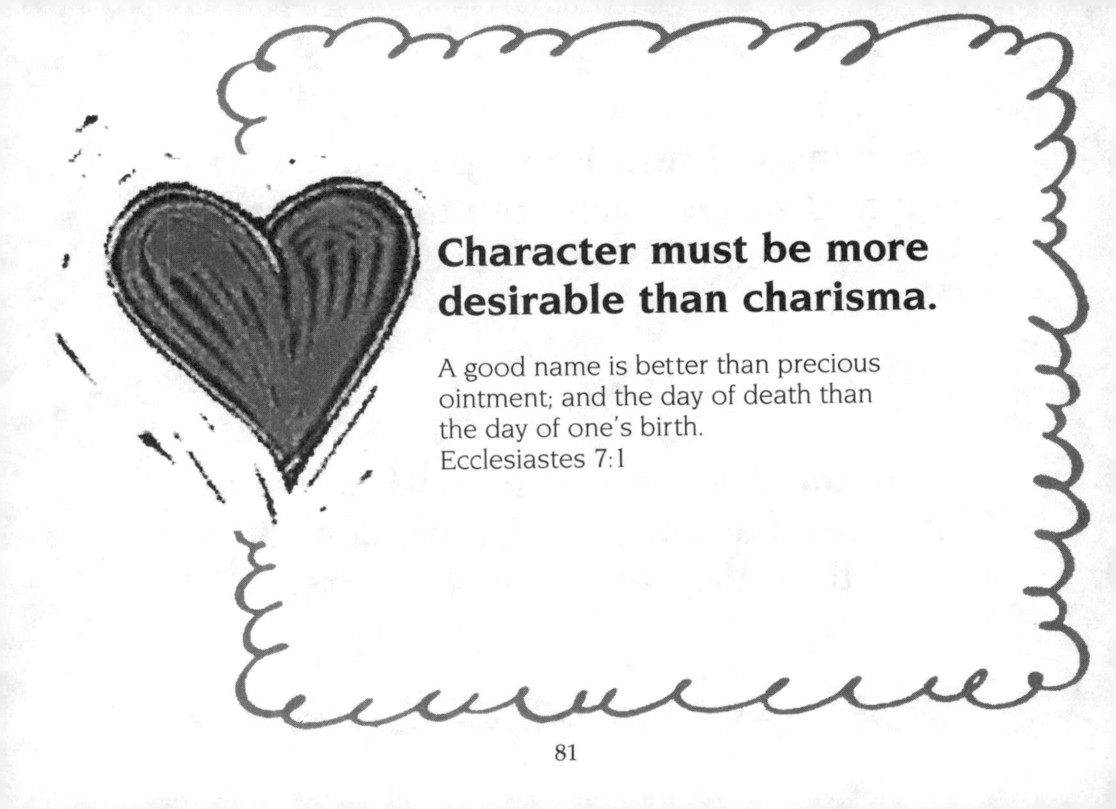

Character must be more desirable than charisma.

A good name is better than precious ointment; and the day of death than the day of one's birth.
Ecclesiastes 7:1

Long-lasting relationships result when men and women are able to respect and accept their differences.

You know you are in love when his or her companionship is more desirable than the company of others.

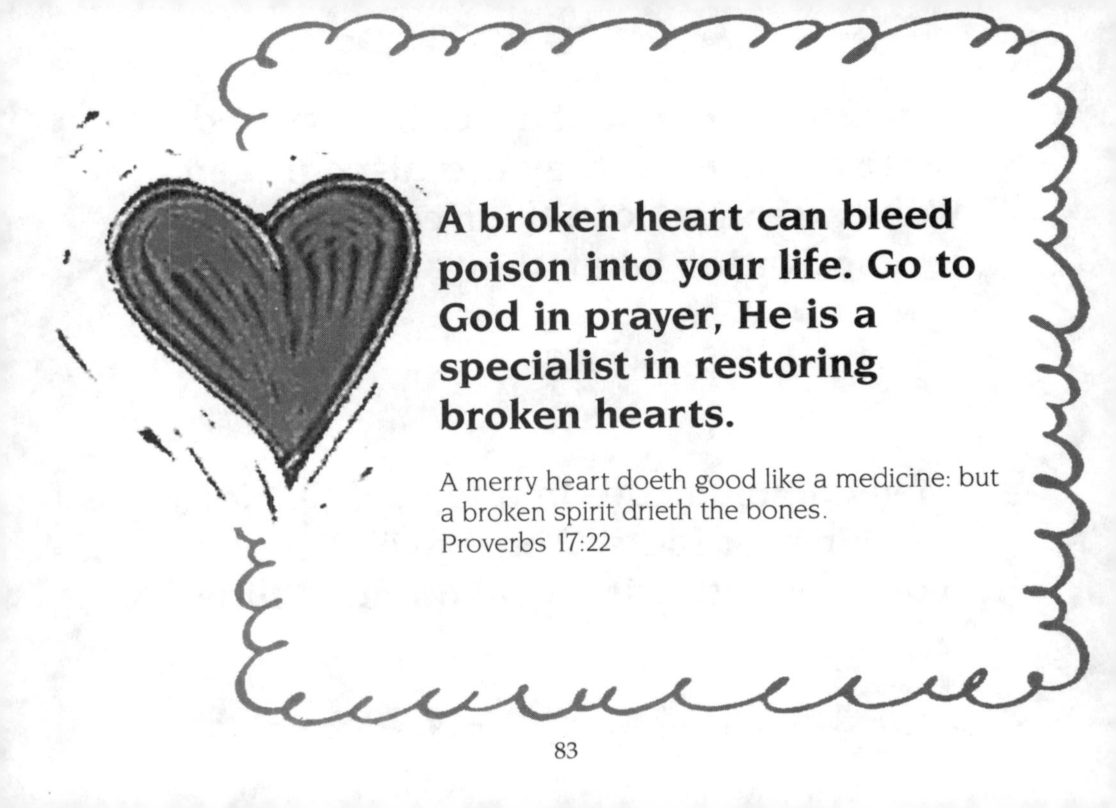

A broken heart can bleed poison into your life. Go to God in prayer, He is a specialist in restoring broken hearts.

A merry heart doeth good like a medicine: but a broken spirit drieth the bones.
Proverbs 17:22

Men tend to lose their creativity and motivation when they are discouraged. Women tend to lose their creativity and motivation when they are lonely.

Men communicate in a logical fashion, looking for facts. Women will usually communicate with insight and feeling.

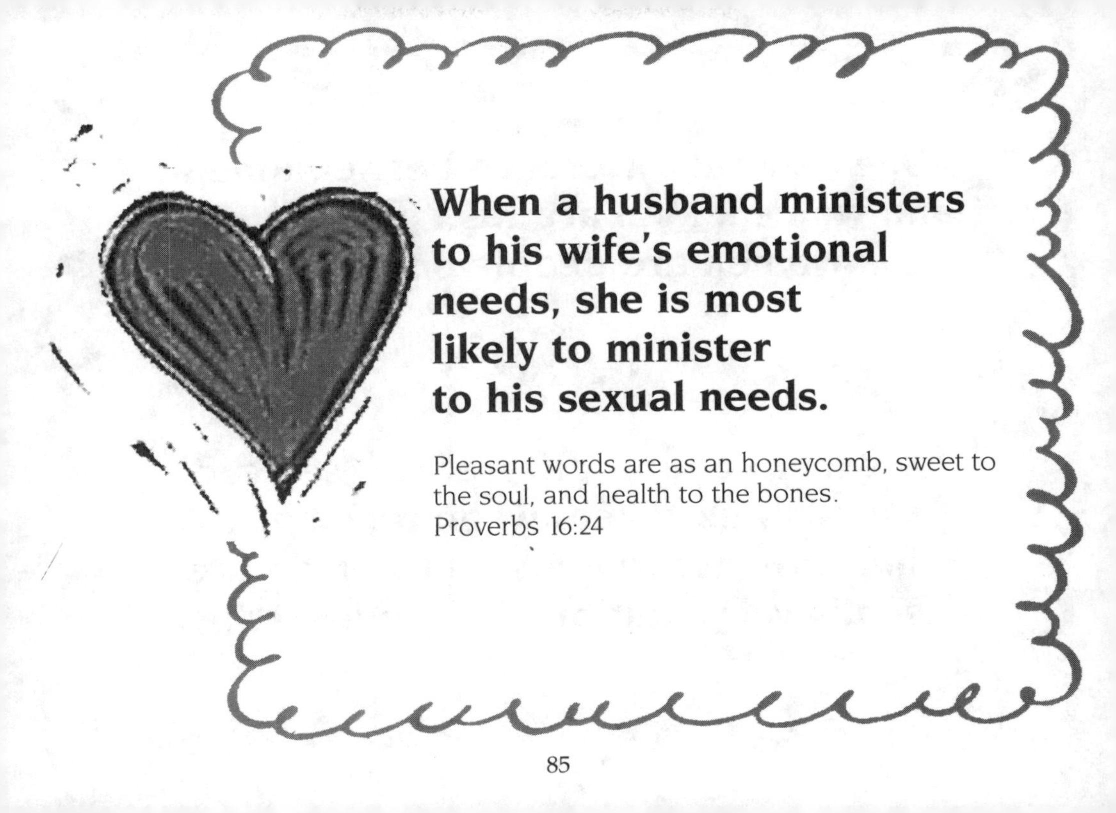

When a husband ministers to his wife's emotional needs, she is most likely to minister to his sexual needs.

Pleasant words are as an honeycomb, sweet to the soul, and health to the bones.
Proverbs 16:24

One general difference between men and women: Men are task oriented and women are people oriented.

Another general difference: Men are usually risk takers when it comes to financial investments and women are usually very cautious before investing.

True friends in a marriage do not insist on having their own way all the time.

Submitting yourselves one to another in the fear of God.
Ephesians 5:21

After the children are born, the pressures and struggles for privacy increase. Therefore, increase your efforts to be alone.

You will enjoy tremendous success in your life if your praise is directed to God, to your mate, and to others.

Accept your mate's nagging habits unconditionally. An amazing thing will happen when you do; those habits will decrease.

Increase your spouse's security by telling him or her, "I love you unconditionally. I will always need you."

A failure to understand the power of praise in a marriage will soon result in failure to have energy for the creativity that every marriage needs.

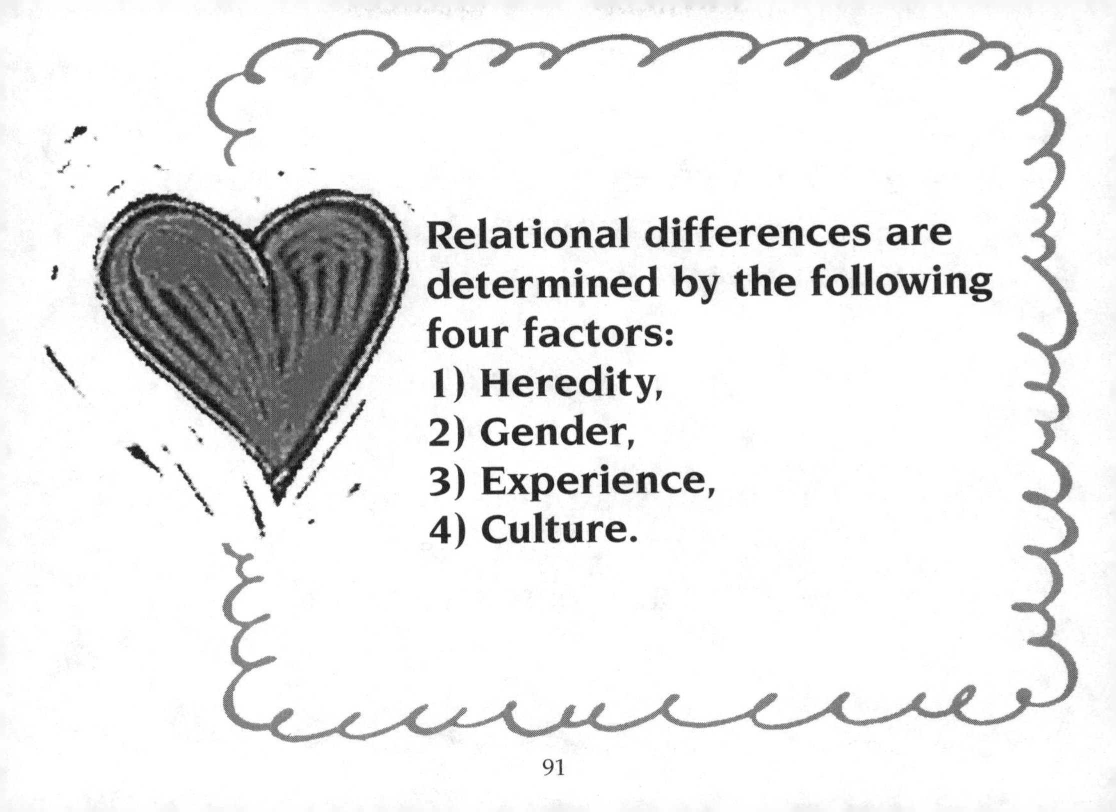

Relational differences are determined by the following four factors:

1) Heredity,

2) Gender,

3) Experience,

4) Culture.

Consider a general difference between men and women: A man is passionate; a woman needs romance.

The most frequent complaint women have about men is that they do not listen to them.

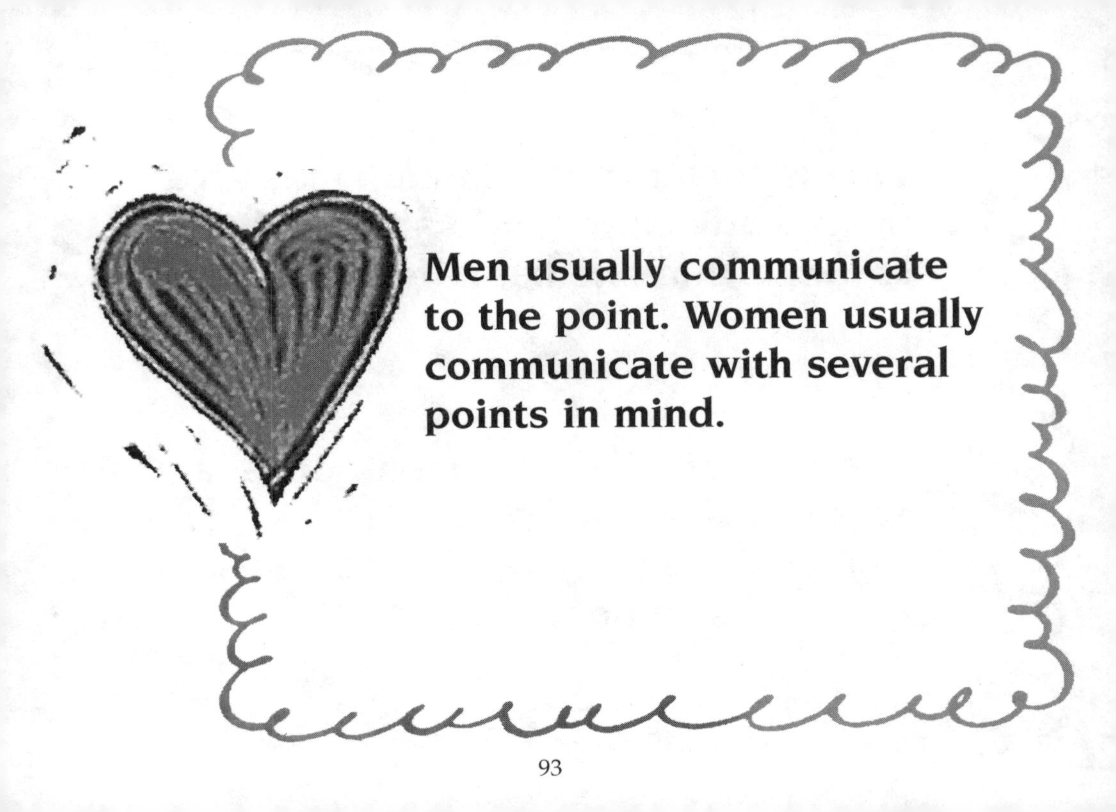

Men usually communicate to the point. Women usually communicate with several points in mind.

Being a nurturer, the woman may give uninvited advice to her husband without knowing that she has offended him.

One of your wife's greatest needs is to know that you have an attentive ear and identify with her feelings and perceptions.

Men usually think they know how to coordinate their dress apparel. They find out differently when they get married!

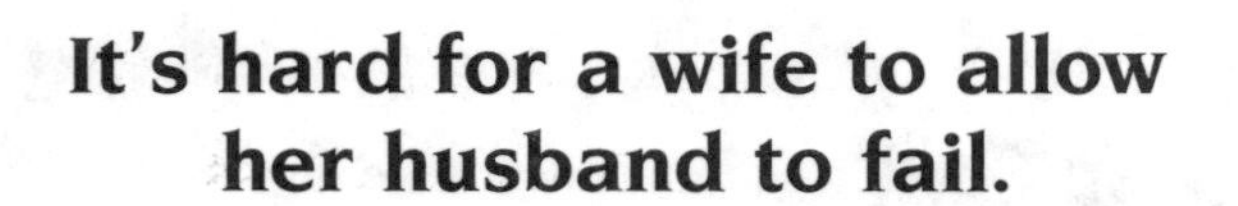

It's hard for a wife to allow her husband to fail.

Friendship in marriage focuses its attention on something besides the other spouse. It involves a mutual interest in the activities of the other partner.

If you respect your spouse, you will treat him or her as an equal.

Let us therefore follow after the things which make for peace, and things wherewith one may edify another.
Romans 14:19

A marriage becomes a friendship when both partners genuinely enjoy each other's company.

True love is being able to overlook your spouse's faults.

Be careful of how you respond to your partner when you are in a hurry or extremely tired.

True friendship is wanting what is best for your mate.

One-sided decisions in a marriage show inconsideration for the feelings of your spouse.

Your spouse will really appreciate it if you clean up your own mess as soon as you have made it.

Learn from each other by becoming both a student and a teacher in your marriage.

Men and women can mean different things by the same statement.

To improve your communication skills, listen first and then ask, "Are you saying...?"

A woman usually pays close attention to the details of a romantic setting — the rose, the candle, the look in her husband's eyes. Let your wife see you looking at her.

Women value greatly the thought behind the gifts they receive from their husbands. A wise husband takes time to think about the gift before he purchases it.

Most couples spend more time and money planning for their wedding than they do preparing for their marriage.

Through wisdom is an house builded; and by understanding it is established. And by knowledge shall the chambers be filled with all precious and pleasant riches.
Proverbs 24:3-4

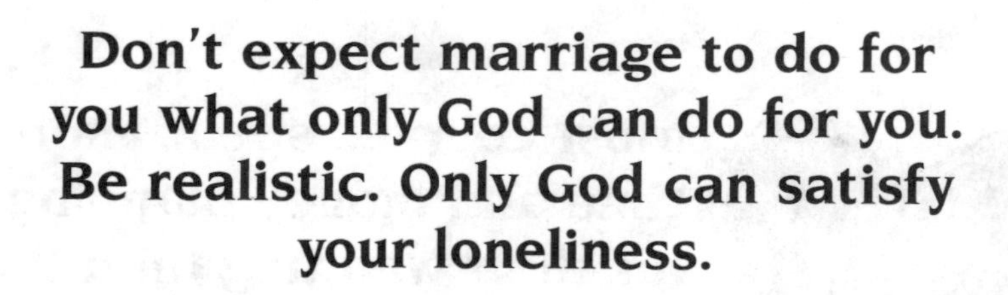

Don't expect marriage to do for you what only God can do for you. Be realistic. Only God can satisfy your loneliness.

When a couple becomes friends, the word "submission" is not in their vocabulary.

Lust looks for ways to get while love looks for ways to give.

For God so loved the world, that he gave his only begotten Son, that whosoever believeth in him should not perish, but have everlasting life.
John 3:16

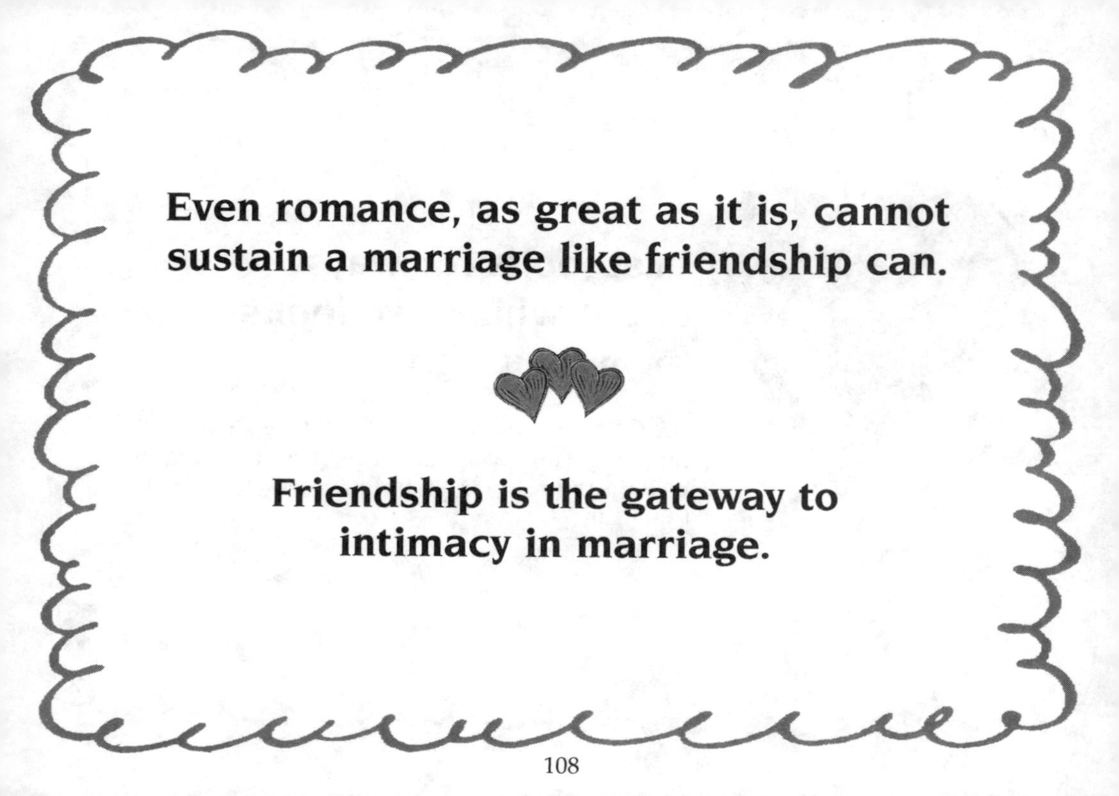

Even romance, as great as it is, cannot sustain a marriage like friendship can.

Friendship is the gateway to intimacy in marriage.

When new ideas are suggested by your spouse, be sympathetic and interested.

And she said unto her husband, Behold now, I perceive that this is an holy man of God, which passeth by us continually.

Let us make a little chamber, I pray thee, on the wall; and let us set for him there a bed, and a table, and a stool, and a candlestick: and it shall be, when he cometh to us, that he shall turn in thither.
2 Kings 4:9-10

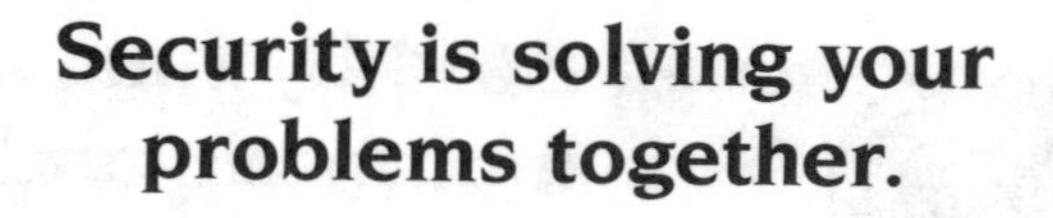

Security is solving your problems together.

It is easier to get married than it is to get a driver's license. However, learning to drive by your spouse's advice can be a real challenge.

Nourish your husband or wife. The word "nourish" means to make great, to keep living, to sustain, to provide, to magnify.

For no man ever yet hated his own flesh;
but nourisheth and cherisheth it,
even as the Lord the church.
Ephesians 5:29

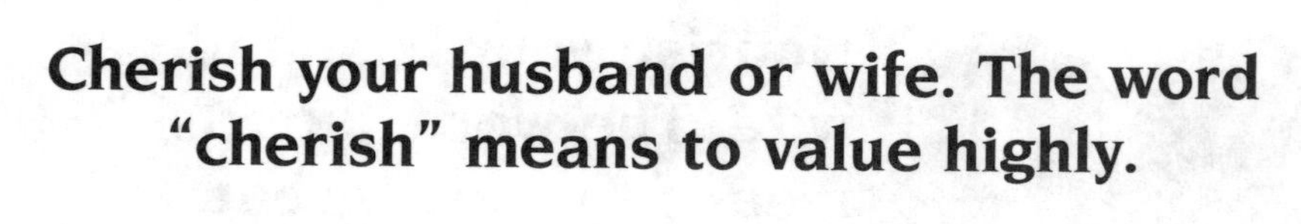

Cherish your husband or wife. The word "cherish" means to value highly.

Your best friend is the one who brings out the best in you.

The power of money can give you an attitude of control. Don't make your spouse feel helpless or subordinate because you bring in the income or earn more money.

Humility looks for actions that deserve praise in another rather than offering criticism.

Positive feedback awaits you from those who are already enjoying a successful marriage.

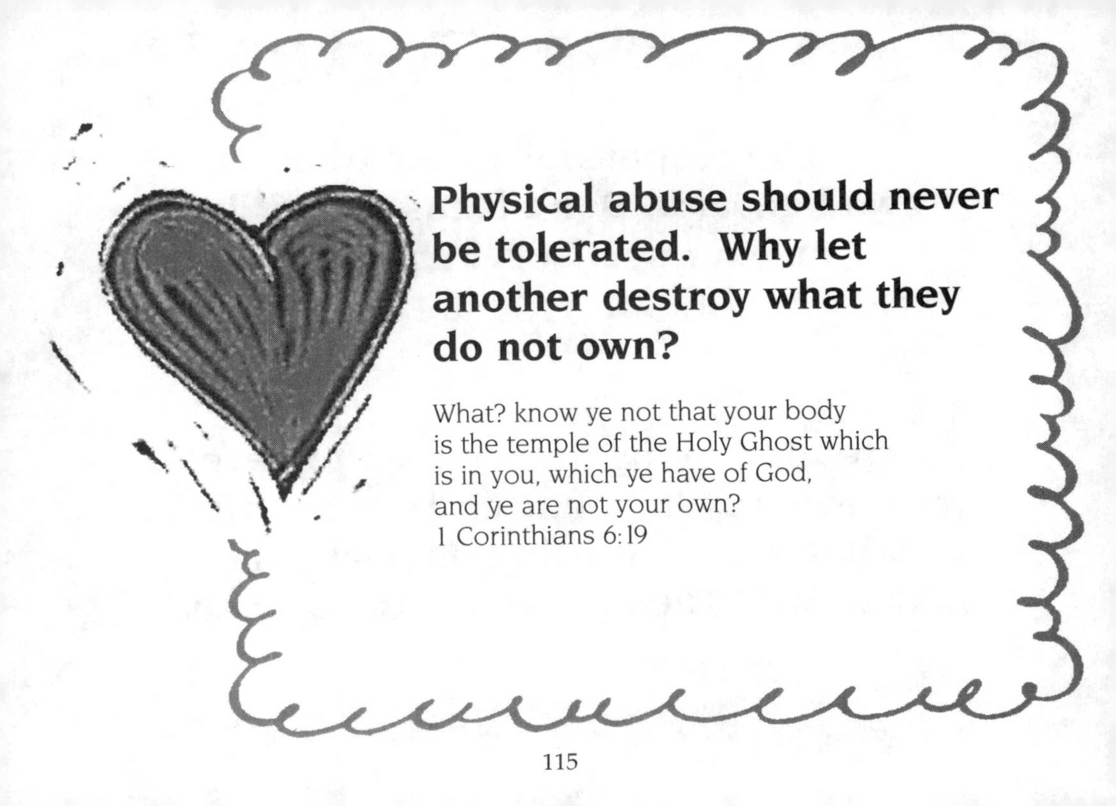

Physical abuse should never be tolerated. Why let another destroy what they do not own?

What? know ye not that your body
is the temple of the Holy Ghost which
is in you, which ye have of God,
and ye are not your own?
1 Corinthians 6:19

Take responsibility for your own behavior. Don't focus primarily on your spouse's behavior.

Instead of being determined to have your own way in a matter, first ask God, "What is Your way in this particular situation?" Then get ready for change.

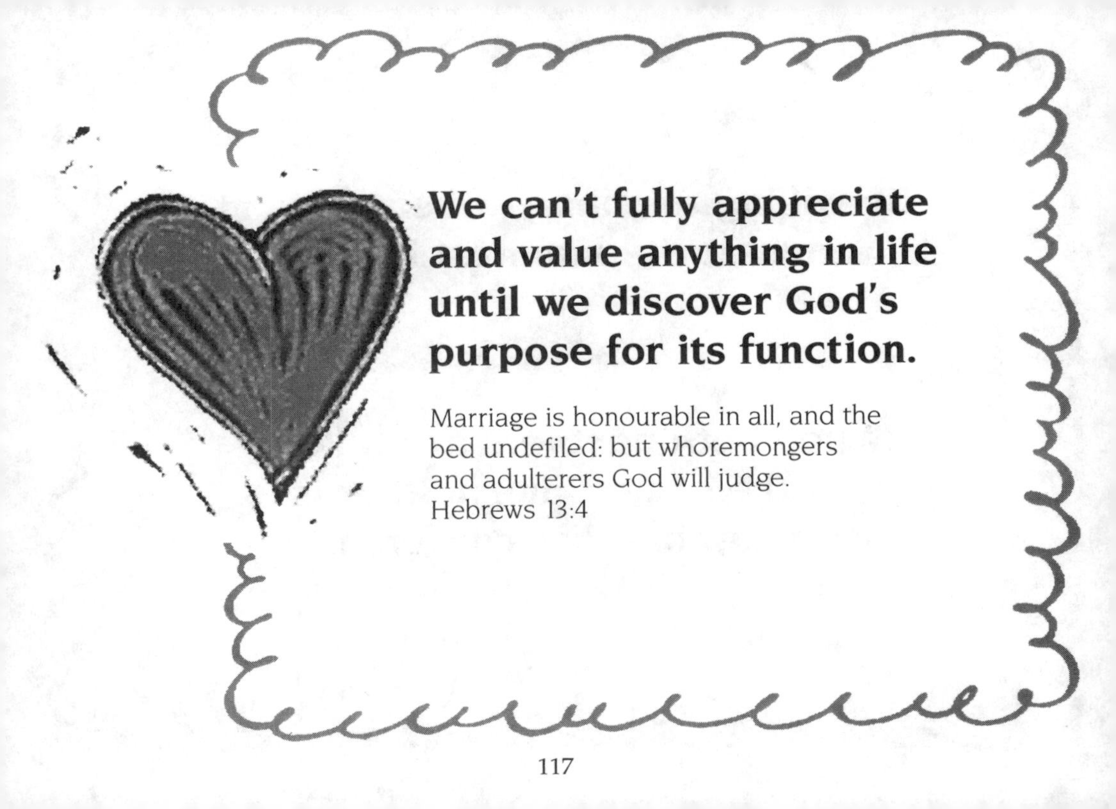

We can't fully appreciate and value anything in life until we discover God's purpose for its function.

Marriage is honourable in all, and the bed undefiled: but whoremongers and adulterers God will judge.
Hebrews 13:4

Be willing to change when signs of immaturity manifest in you.

When both partners are talking at the same time, neither is listening to either conversation.

A marriage of strength and unity consists of three partners: the man, the woman, and Christ.

And if one prevail against him,
two shall withstand him; and a
threefold cord is not quickly broken.
Ecclesiastes 4:12b

Return quickly to the "Interstate of Love" when you have mistakenly taken the exit of "Indifference and Strife."

When a husband feels His wife is burdening him with unnecessary information, he would do well to ask her to repeat what she just said.

If you married just to get away from home, you are most likely not going to enjoy your new home.

Therefore shall a man leave his father and his mother, and shall cleave unto his wife: and they shall be one flesh.
Genesis 2:24

A problem left alone will grow into a larger problem that will drain the life out of your marriage. Confront the situation with a well thought-out solution.

Men and women have the same needs for self-worth and belonging. They satisfy these needs in different fashions.

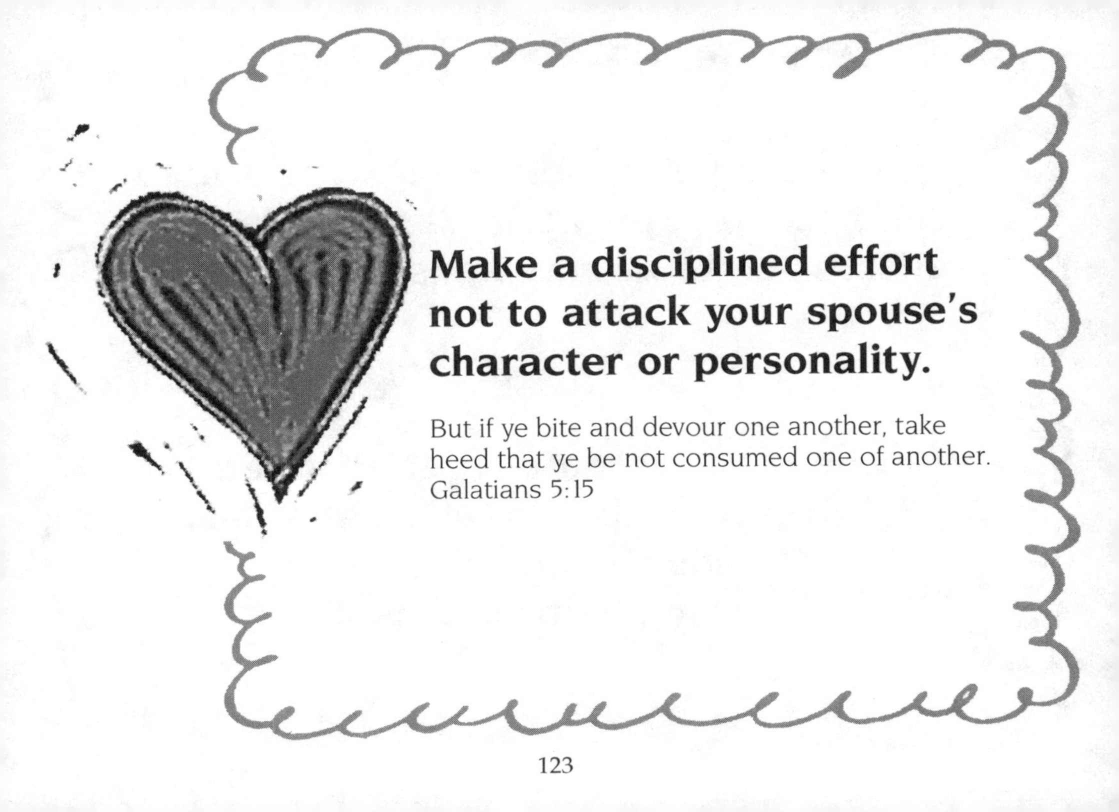

Make a disciplined effort not to attack your spouse's character or personality.

But if ye bite and devour one another, take heed that ye be not consumed one of another.
Galatians 5:15

If there is a potentially explosive issue to be discussed, pray together before the discussion to avoid extensive damage.

One of the rare discoveries in life is when a husband realizes that his wife has simple solutions to complex problems.

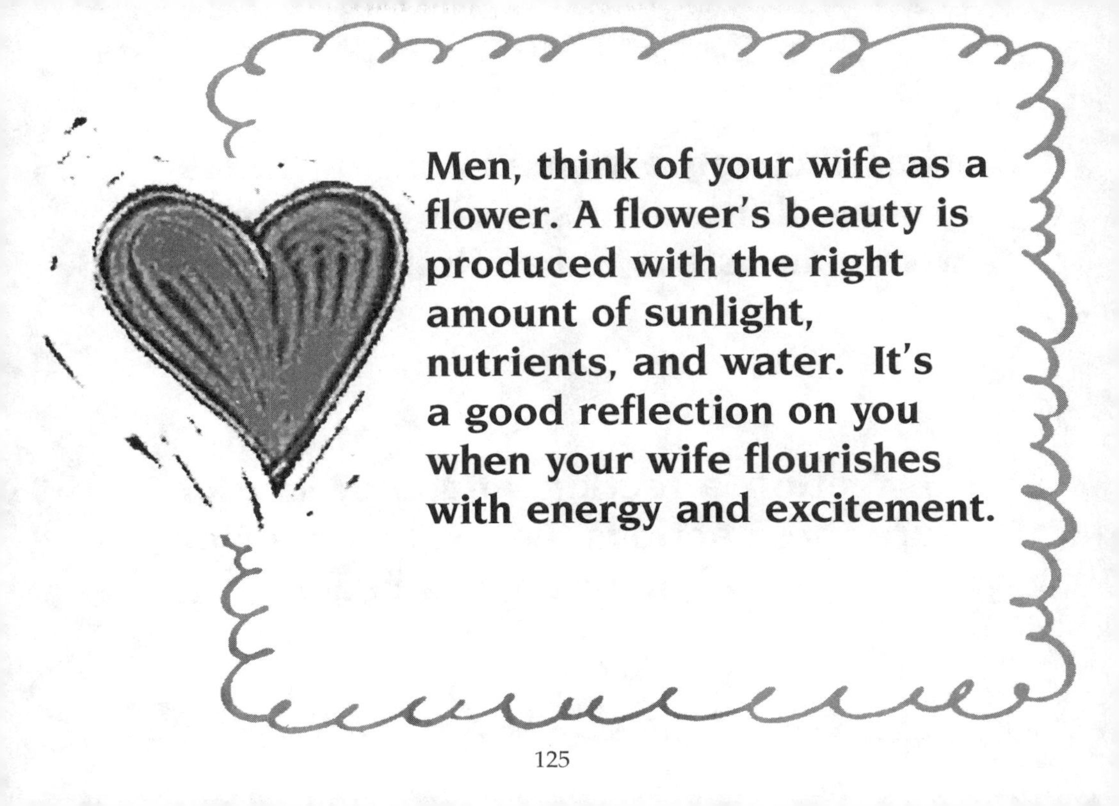

Men, think of your wife as a flower. A flower's beauty is produced with the right amount of sunlight, nutrients, and water. It's a good reflection on you when your wife flourishes with energy and excitement.

Instinctively a woman feels or knows some things that she can't explain. A wise man listens to her first impressions.

Attention, affection, and appreciation are three actions that will gain a man an "A" in a woman's heart.

We are fearfully and wonderfully made. Our body parts as husbands and wives have been detailed by God to provide for intense pleasure in intimate contact.

I will praise thee; for I am fearfully and wonderfully made: marvellous are thy works; and that my soul knoweth right well.
Psalms 139:14

Listen to yourself as you speak. If you don't like what you are saying or the way you are saying it, the person listening is probably not being edified either.

A "low blow" in boxing refers to hitting below the belt. A "low blow" in marriage is when one partner says something to his or her spouse that will intentionally hurt.

The wife is more likely to nurture a relationship because there is an "instinctive awareness" of what a relationship should be.

Men are more violent than women when they are angry. Women are more verbal when they are angry.

"Listening love" means that you have the ability to let the other partner speak without interruption.

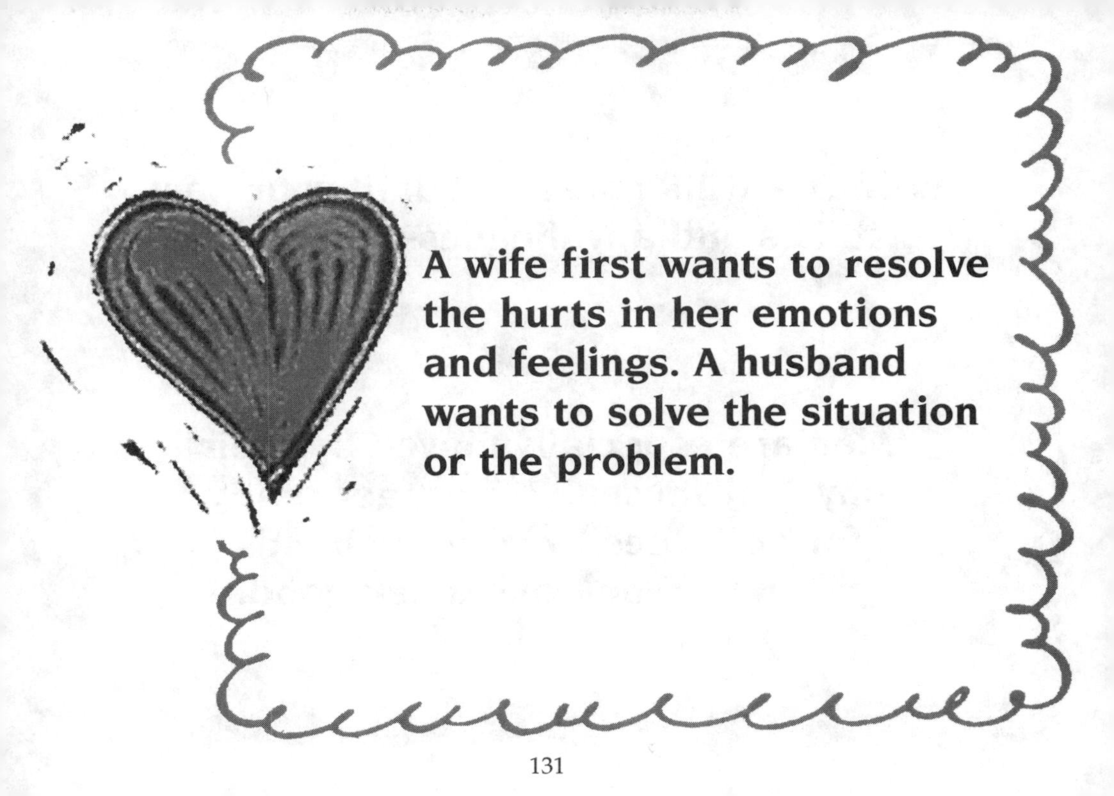

A wife first wants to resolve the hurts in her emotions and feelings. A husband wants to solve the situation or the problem.

Love is a willingness to admit your past mistakes and a willingness to improve.

Men are especially moved by their physical senses. Wives, get ready for advances by your husbands when you look and smell good.

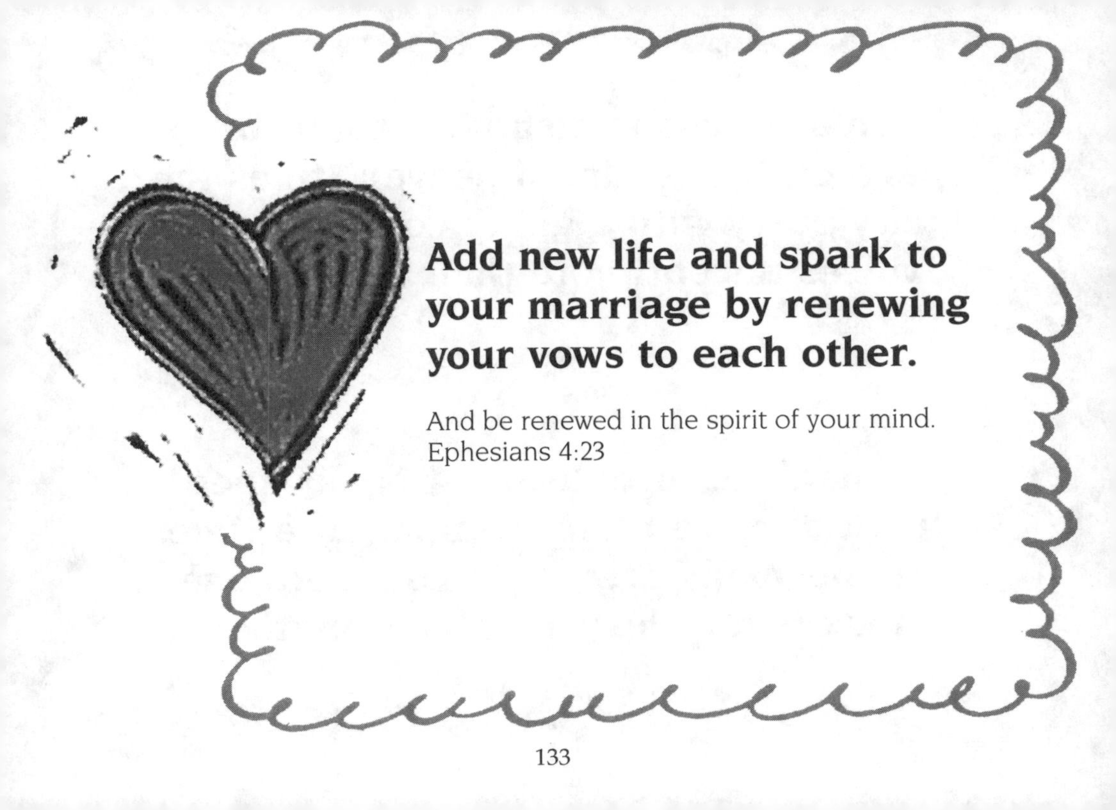

Add new life and spark to your marriage by renewing your vows to each other.

And be renewed in the spirit of your mind.
Ephesians 4:23

When a spouse is dishonest to his or her partner, the "court of heaven" fines the guilty party with a guilty conscience that voices deception to their heart daily.

A man's nature does not easily keep track of more than one thing at a time. He normally prefers to complete one task before hearing about another.

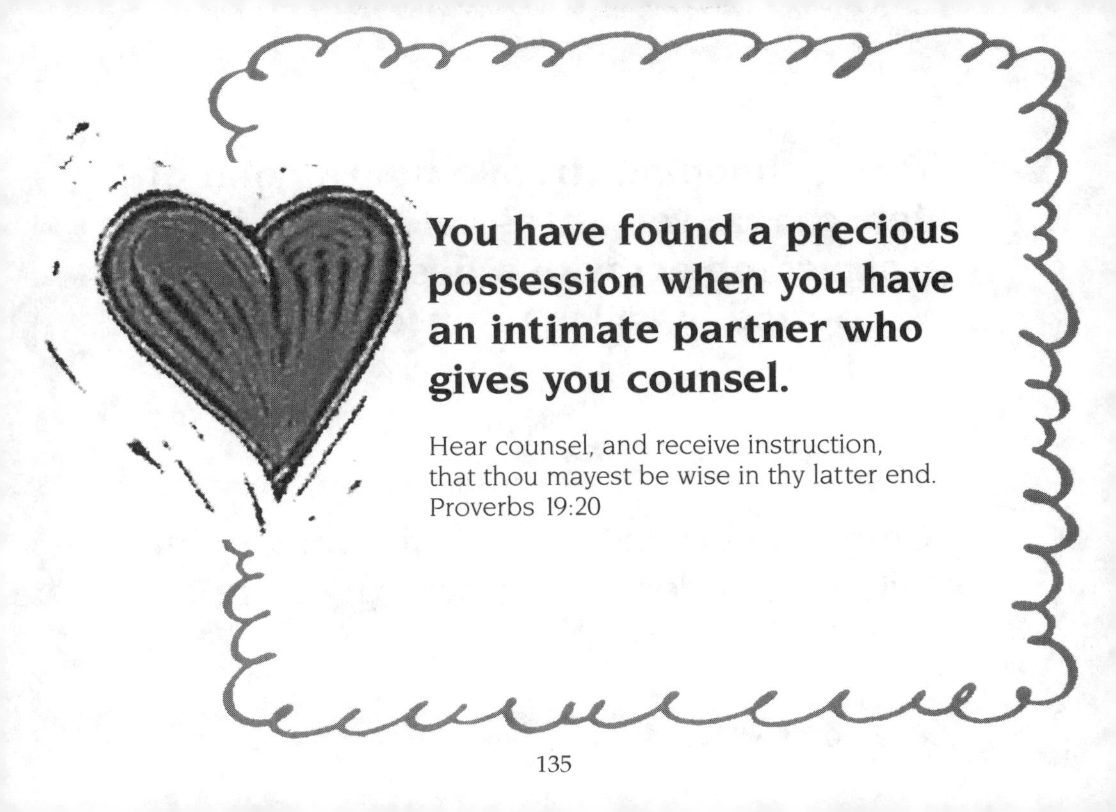

You have found a precious possession when you have an intimate partner who gives you counsel.

Hear counsel, and receive instruction,
that thou mayest be wise in thy latter end.
Proverbs 19:20

"Going shopping" from a man's point of view can be very stressful if there is no assigned object with a designated time period in which to purchase it.

"Going shopping" from a woman's point of view provides an opportunity to relax.

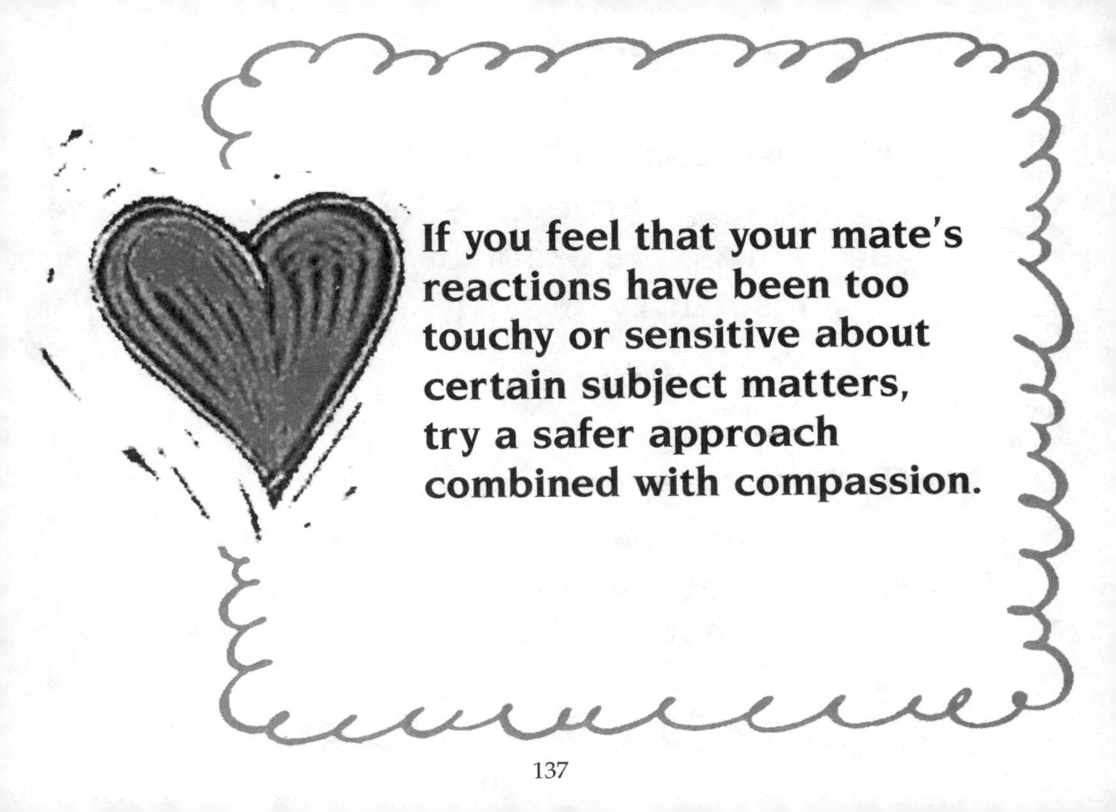

If you feel that your mate's reactions have been too touchy or sensitive about certain subject matters, try a safer approach combined with compassion.

When we don't reach out and meet each other's needs as husbands and wives, the problem is usually insecurity or selfishness.

Don't re-open each other's wounds by using afflicting words or you may soon find yourself in a marital fight that can't be won.

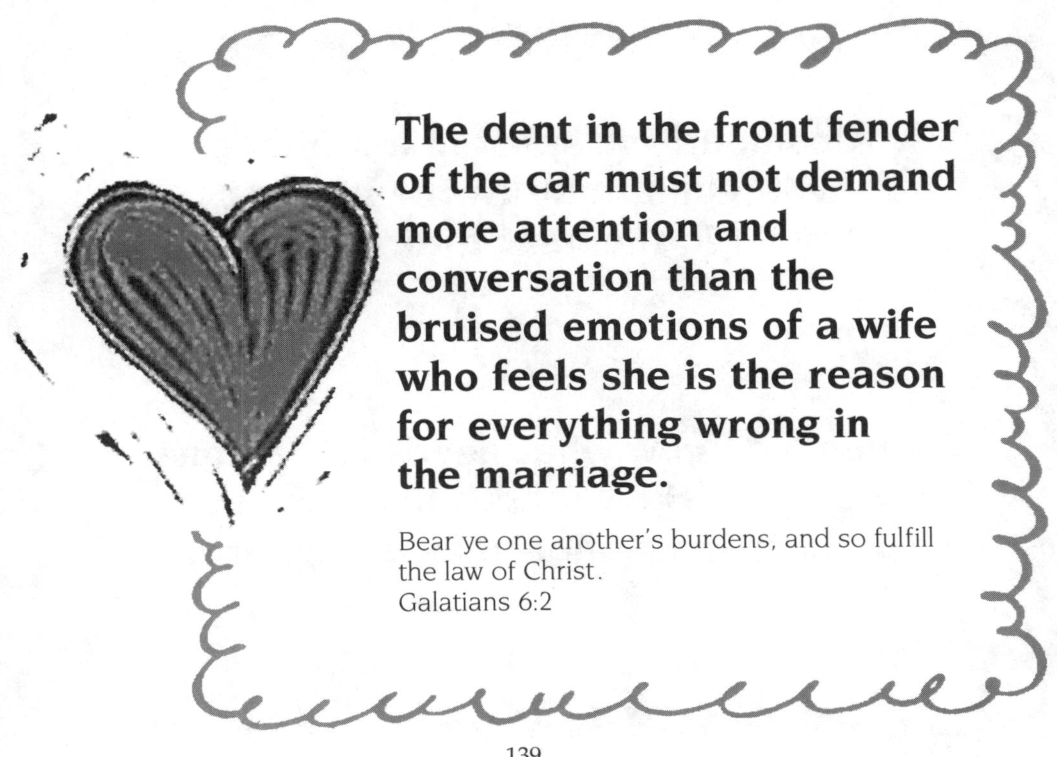

The dent in the front fender of the car must not demand more attention and conversation than the bruised emotions of a wife who feels she is the reason for everything wrong in the marriage.

Bear ye one another's burdens, and so fulfill the law of Christ.
Galatians 6:2

A competitive spirit in a marriage will result in a divorce hearing in the near future.

When we know what needs to be done, we can make changes that produce a marriage of harmony and peace.

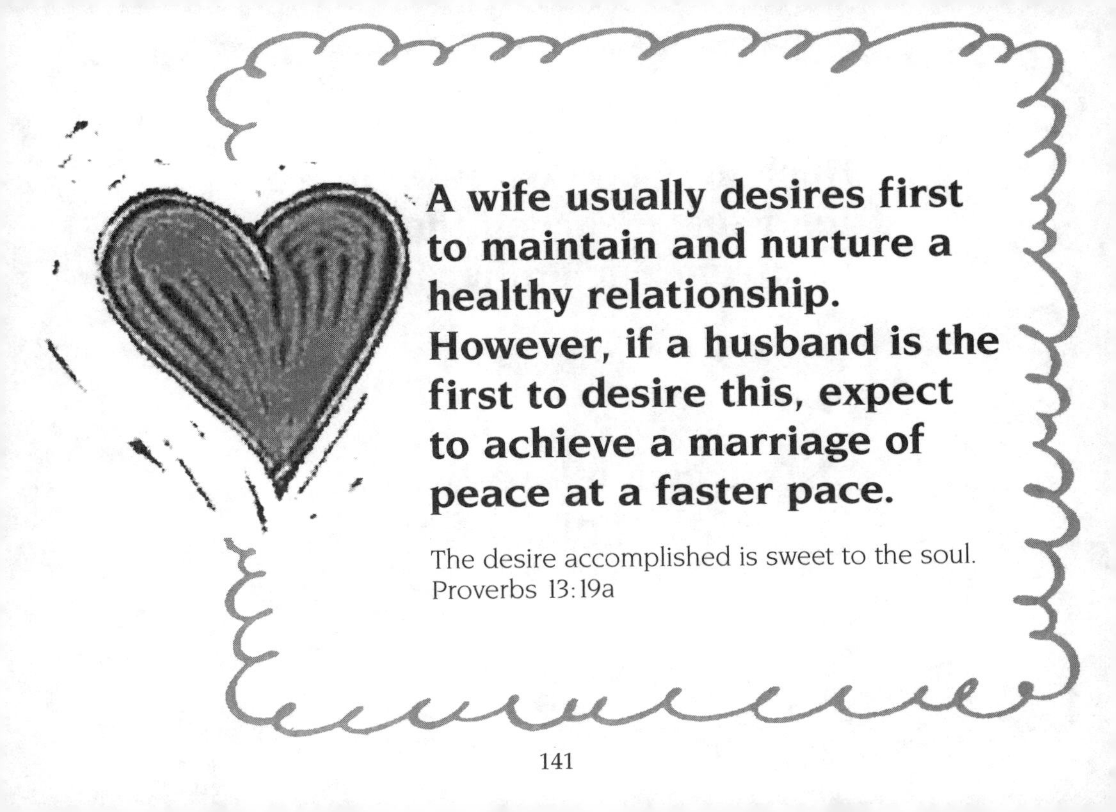

A wife usually desires first to maintain and nurture a healthy relationship. However, if a husband is the first to desire this, expect to achieve a marriage of peace at a faster pace.

The desire accomplished is sweet to the soul.
Proverbs 13:19a

Husbands and wives who are friends have earned the right to confront each other in love.

Friendship loves with a high appreciation.

Men, if you think that your responsibilities end when you leave your job, think again. Ask your wife, "Can I help you or assist you in any way?"

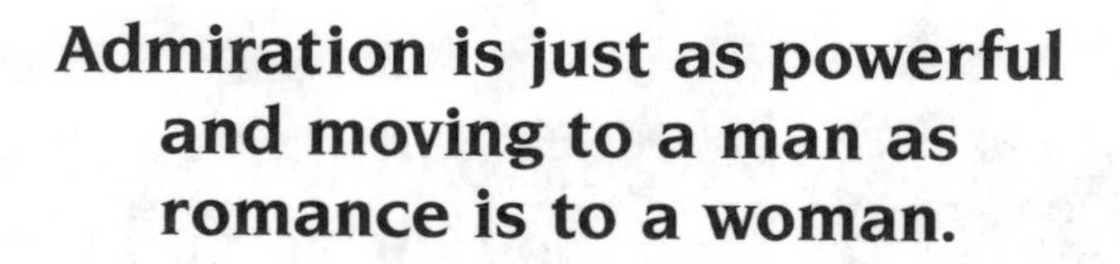

Admiration is just as powerful and moving to a man as romance is to a woman.

A critical spirit demonstrated by either partner will rarely produce an atmosphere conducive to change.

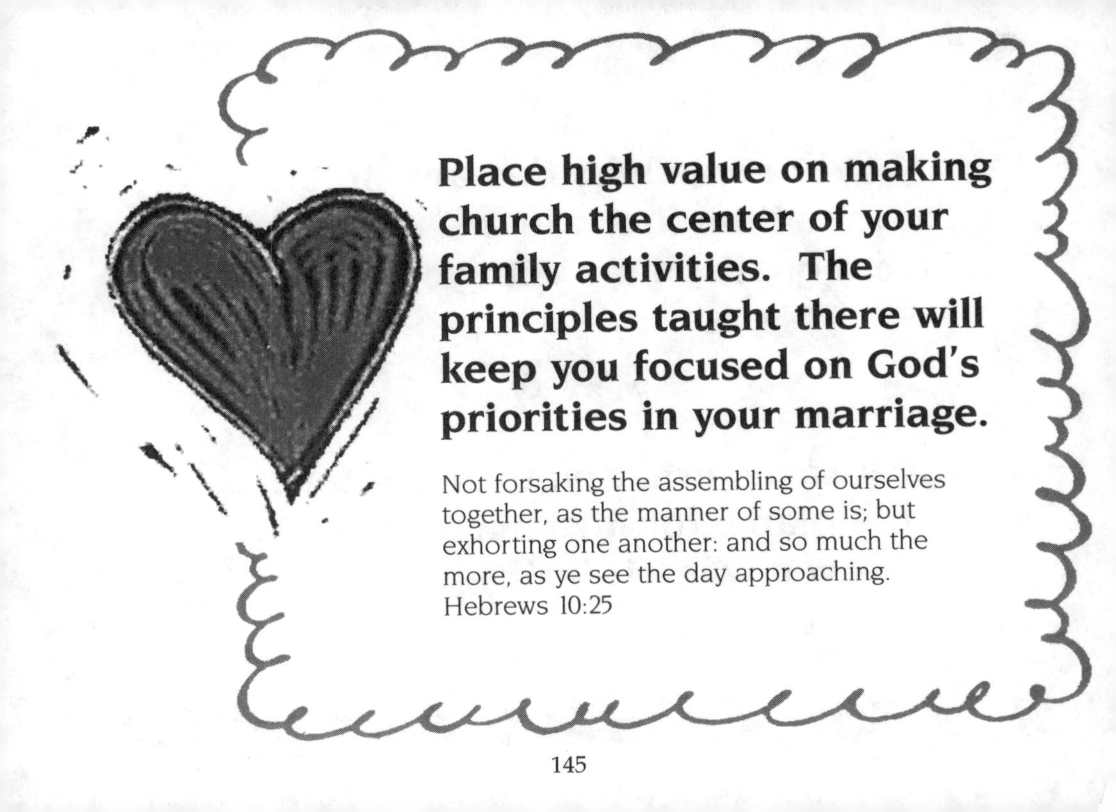

Place high value on making church the center of your family activities. The principles taught there will keep you focused on God's priorities in your marriage.

Not forsaking the assembling of ourselves together, as the manner of some is; but exhorting one another: and so much the more, as ye see the day approaching.
Hebrews 10:25

Avoid people who demand so much of your time that you are taken away from quality time with your spouse.

It takes great maturity to take the blame for miscommunication, even when it isn't your fault.

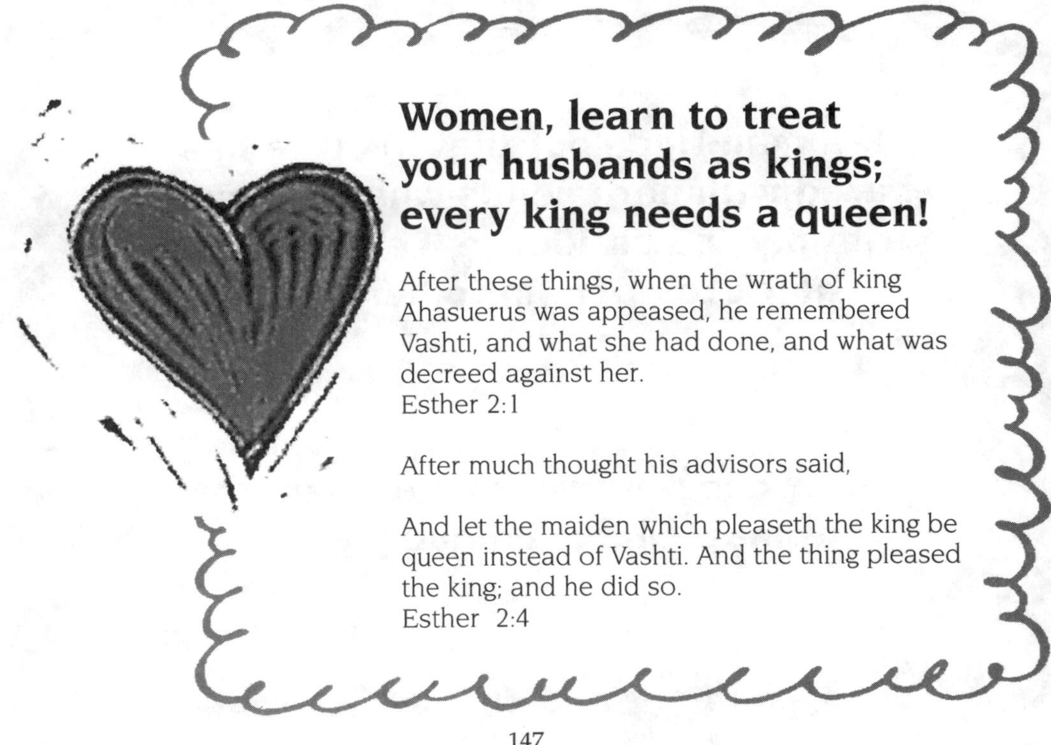

Women, learn to treat your husbands as kings; every king needs a queen!

After these things, when the wrath of king Ahasuerus was appeased, he remembered Vashti, and what she had done, and what was decreed against her.
Esther 2:1

After much thought his advisors said,

And let the maiden which pleaseth the king be queen instead of Vashti. And the thing pleased the king; and he did so.
Esther 2:4

If a man finds out that his wife has shared with her friends what he shared with her in confidence, he will not be quick to open up to her again.

Never compare your wife to another woman. She is uniquely yours!

Good and bad marriages will encounter conflicts and disagreements. The goal in such times of intense fellowship should be to find a workable solution without a broken spirit.

Making love is more than physical; it is the desire to satisfy your marriage partner.

Marriage grows better with love.

Cars, clothes, houses, or money cannot fill the void in our lives like a loving relationship with our spouse. However, you do need all of the above as accessories.

When you have a fight with your spouse, it's probably because neither of you are feeling loved or understood.

Submitting to each other's ideas is a great instrument for developing your character.

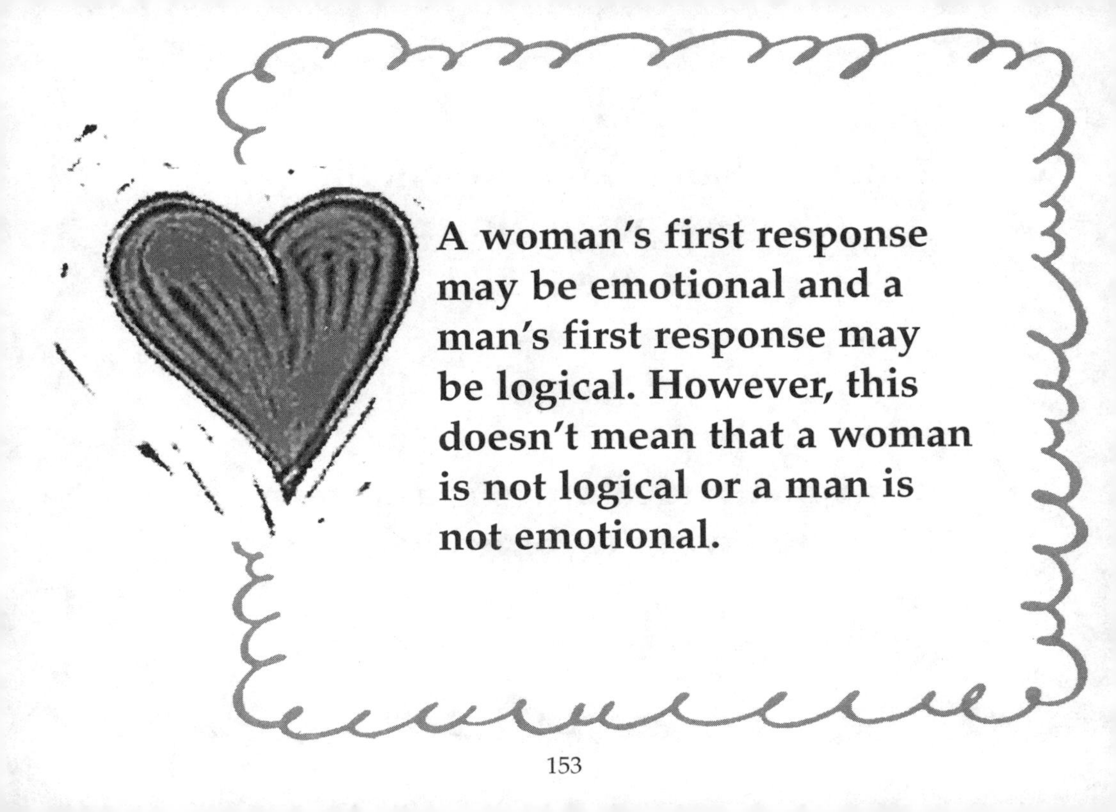

A woman's first response may be emotional and a man's first response may be logical. However, this doesn't mean that a woman is not logical or a man is not emotional.

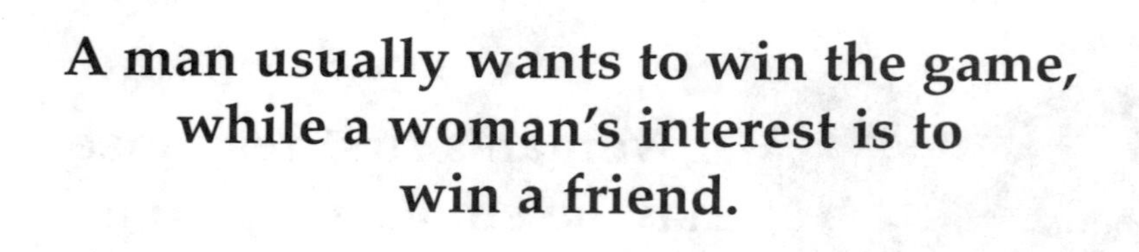

A man usually wants to win the game, while a woman's interest is to win a friend.

A man's ideal mate is a woman who loves the things he loves.

When an extrovert marries an introvert, extreme caution is needed when expressing extreme suggestions to each other.

About the Authors

Dr. Mack Timberlake, Jr., is pastor of Christian Faith Center in Creedmoor, North Carolina, from where, through diversified methods of television, radio, books, and tapes, the Word of God is launched forth all over the world.

He and his wife, Brenda, minister uniquely together to couples in seminars and by way of their national television program which is seen daily on several national networks.

To contact the authors, write:

Mack and Brenda Timberlake
Christian Faith Center
101 S. Peachtree Street
P. O. Box 100
Creedmoor, NC 27522

Tel.: 919-528-1581
Fax: 919-528-3816

Other Books
by Mack and Brenda Timberlake

When the Wine
Runs Out of Your Marriage

Heaven on Earth in Your Marriage

Understanding Male and Female
Relationships

Additional copies of this book
are available from your local bookstore.

Harrison House
Tulsa, Oklahoma 74153

In Canada books are available from:
Word Alive • P.O. Box 670
Niverville, Manitoba
CANADA ROA 1EO

The Harrison House Vision

Proclaiming the truth and the power
Of the Gospel of Jesus Christ
With excellence;

Challenging Christians to
Live victoriously,
Grow spiritually,
Know God intimately